RAILWAY STATIONS
of
WESTERN CANADA

THE RAILWAY STATIONS
OF WESTERN CANADA

an architectural history by

J. EDWARD MARTIN

STUDIO E

British Columbia, Canada.

Designed and published by Studio E Martin,
White Rock, B.C., Canada. V4B 4B2

Printed in Canada

ISBN 0-920716-00-8

FOREWORD

If this volume accomplishes some small increase in the understanding, appreciation and enjoyment of this very vital segment of the Canadian architectural heritage, its long and painstaking production will have been worthwhile.

The author would like to thank the railway companies, as well as the numerous architects, engineers, station operators, archivists and librarians whose cooperation, kindness and interest during the making of this book have been much appreciated. The Canada Council deserves special recognition for its support through the Explorations Programme, which enabled the requisite extensive research to be carried out. And finally, to the many friends who inspired, constructively criticized, or morally supported the project, many, many thanks.

White Rock, B.C.,
Autumn, 1979.

Detail of Central Gables, CPR Medicine Hat II.

CONTENTS

Foreword v
List of Illustrations viii

PART I: 1875-1900

Centrum   3
The First Wave   7
The Grand Manner 14
Minor Stations of the 1890s 22

PART II: 1900-1940

Introductory History 30
Manitoba Classics 33
Competition's Spur 38
Vancouver Triad 46
The Canadian Northern Family 53
The Grand Trunk Pacific Family 65
The Smaller Railways 71
Developments After 1920 78

PART III: 1940-1980

The New Era 94
Canadian Pacific Streamlines 97
Canadian National Modernizes 99
New PGE and NAR Terminals 105
All Aboard! 109

Notes to the Text 112
Bibliography 114
Index 115

LIST OF ILLUSTRATIONS

Frontispieces: Detail of CPR Medicine Hat II central gables; Leaded windows of CPR Lake Louise (1909) general waiting room.

1. Meeting the Train, Medicine Hat, Alberta, c.1890. *Glenbow Museum Archives, Calgary.*
2. Sandford Fleming's Proposed Standard Town Plan (1877).
3. Common Site Patterns: a) Moose Jaw, Sask. b) Beiseker, Alta.
4. Portable CPR Station of the 1880s. Track and End Elevations.
5. Standard Canadian Pacific Railway Station at Gleichen, Alberta. *Glenbow Museum Archives.*
6. CPR Medicine Hat (1883). Track Elevation & Ground Floor Plan.
7. First CPR Station at Winnipeg, Manitoba (1882). *Provincial Archives of Manitoba.*
8. CPR Log Station at Laggan, Alberta (1886). *Provincial Archives of Alberta, E. Brown Collection.*
9. Roger's Pass, British Columbia. Selkirk Mountain Range. *Public Archives of Canada C5303.*
10. CPR Glacier House, British Columbia (1886). *Public Archives of Canada 25040.*
11. Northern Pacific Railway's Winnipeg Station-Hotel (1892). *Provincial Archives of Manitoba.*
12. Canadian Pacific Railway Station at Regina, Saskatchewan (1892). *Public Archives of Canada 48275*
13. Second CPR Calgary Station (1893). *Provincial Archives of Alberta, E. Brown Collection.*
14. CPR Vancouver Terminal (1898) by Edward Maxwell. *Public Archives of Canada 31666.*
15. CPR Station-Hotel at Moose Jaw, Sask. (1898) by E. Maxwell. *Public Archives of Canada 29399.*
16. Maxwell's CPR Station-Hotel for Sicamous, B.C. (1898). *Public Archives of Canada 32020.*
17. Canadian Pacific's New Westminster, B.C. (1899) by E. Maxwell.
18. Detail of Masonry, CPR New Westminster, B.C. (1899).
19. CPR Agassiz, B.C. (1893) as it appeared in the 1970s.
20. Original Window Sash on CPR Agassiz (1893).
21. Cross Section of a Wall with Drop Siding.
22. CPR Virden, Manitoba (1899) by R. B. Pratt. Built 1906.
23. Ground Floor Plan, CPR Virden, Manitoba (1899).
24. CPR Shelter at Moberly, British Columbia (c.1893).
25. Innisfail, Alberta, Calgary & Edmonton Railway (1891). *Glenbow Museum Archives.*
26. Shuswap & Okanagan (CPR) Station at Armstrong, B.C. (1892).
27. CPR Crow's Nest Branch Standard 2nd Class Station (1898).
28. Winnipeg CPR II (1904) by W.S. and E. Maxwell. *Public Archives of Canada 9455.*
29. Winnipeg Union Station (1911) by Warren & Wetmore. *Public Archives of Canada 21730.*
30. Restaurant Entrance, Winnipeg Union Station (1911).
31. Plan of Main Floor, Winnipeg Union Station (1911).
32. CNR Brandon, Manitoba (1911) with Prince Edward Hotel at right.
33. Canadian Pacific's Brandon, Manitoba Station (1911).
34. Canadian Northern Railway's Edmonton Station (1905). *Provincial Archives of Alberta, E. Brown Collection.*
35. Canadian Pacific's Red Deer, Alberta Station (1910).
36. CPR's Second Banff Station (1910). *Photo Canadian Pacific.*
37. CPR Wilkie, Saskatchewan (1906-08).
38. Canadian Pacific's Vernon, British Columbia Station (1911).
39. CPR Standard Number Five Station at Bow Island, Alta. (1911).
40. Calgary CPR II (1908) with the Royla Visit of 1939. *Glenbow Museum Archives.*
41. Canadian Northern's Calgary Terminal (1905-16). *Glenbow Museum Archives.*
42. Union Station at Portage la Prairie, Manitoba (1908). *Public Archives of Canada 21204.*
43. Vancouver, CPR III (1912-14) by Barrott, Blackader & Webster.
44. General Waiting Room and Lobby of Vancouver CPR III.
45. Track Side of Vancouver CPR III.

46. Great Northern's Union Station, Vancouver, B.C. (1915) by F. L. Townley.
47. Plan of Main Floor, CNR Vancouver (1919).
48. Vancouver, B.C., CNR Terminal (1916-19) by R. B. Pratt. *Public Archives of Canada 49733.*
49. Ornamental Plaster Ceiling, General Waiting Room, CNR Vancouver.
50. Modern Butterfly Type Platform Covers, CNR Vancouver.
51. Canadian Northern's Laurier, Manitoba (1899). *Manitoba Provincial Archives.*
52. Canadian Northern Combined Station-Section House (1900).
53. Floor Plans of CNR Combined Station-Section House (1900).
54. Canadian Northern Station for St. Boniface and Ft. Frances (1901). Track and End Elevations, Plan and Cross Section.
55. Canadian Northern's Vermilion, Alberta (1906). Street Side. *Public Archives of Canada 11512.*
56. CNR Stettler, Alberta (1911). Track Side.
57. Canadian Northern Standard 3rd Class Depot (1901 Version).
58. CNR 3rd Class Depot (revised type) at Smoky Lake, Alberta (1919).
59. Ground Floor Plan of CNR St. Paul, Alberta (1921).
60. CNR 1912 Combined Station-Section House at Galloway, Alta. (1913).
61. Ground Floor Plan, CNR 1912 Combined Station-Section House.
62. CNR Chilliwack, B.C. (1915) by John Schofield.
63. Standard Canadian Northern Station Bench.
64. Grand Trunk Pacific Railway's Melville, Saskatchewan (1909). *Public Archives of Canada 21218.*
65. GTPR's Wainwright, Alberta (1909, destroyed by fire 1929). *Glenbow Museum Archives.*
66. Grand Trunk Pacific's Unity, Saskatchewan (1909-10).
67. GTPR Eaves Supports (c.1910).
68. Eaves Brackets, GTR Ernestown, Ontario (c.1854).
69. GTPR Standard Station at Nokomis, Saskatchewan (1907). *Public Archives of Canada 21228.*
70. GTPR Standard Design A Station (1910) at Coleville, Sask. *Provincial Archives of Alberta, Pollard Collection.*
71. GTPR Standard Design A Floor Plans (1910).
72. Grand Trunk Pacific's Three Hills, Alberta (1919).
73. Esquimalt & Nanaimo Railway's Nanaimo, B.C. Station (1920).
74. E&NR Station at Parksville, British Columbia (1911).
75. Main BCER Terminal in Vancouver (1911) by Somervell & Putnam. *Photo BC Hydro.*
76. BCER Lulu Island Line Terminal in Vancouver (1913). *Photo BC Hydro.*
77. White Pass & Yukon Railway's Whitehorse Station (1900). *Photo Canadian Pacific.*
78. ED&BCR's Standard Depot at Berwyn, Alberta (1922).
79. Pacific Great Eastern's Clinton, B.C. Station (1915).
80. Canadian Pacific's Moose Jaw, Sask. (1920) by Hugh G. Jones.
81. General Waiting Room, CPR Moose Jaw, Saskatchewan (1920).
82. Jasper, Alberta, Canadian National Railways' Station of 1925.
83. CNR Edmonton, Alberta (1928). Ground Floor Plan.
84. Union Station at Regina, Saskatchewan (1931).
85. Waiting Room, Regina Union Station (1931).
86. CPR West Summerland, B.C. (1923).
87. CNR Kamloops, British Columbia (1926).
88. CPR Lloydminster, Saskatchewan (1927).
89. Canadian National Railways' Le Pas, Manitoba (1928).
90. GWWDR St. Boniface, Manitoba (1929).
91. Canadian National Railways' Vegreville, Alberta (1930).
92. Detail of West End, CNR Vegreville (1930).
93. CNR Western Lines 3rd Class Station (1929) at Scott, Sask.
94. CNR Western Lines 4th Class Station (1929) at Denholm, Sask.
95. CPR Western Lines 16A Station (1928) at Neilburg, Saskatchewan.
96. CPR Western Lines 16A Station, Ground and Upper Floor Plans.

97. Canadian Pacific Railway's Penticton, B.C. (1941-46).
98. Under Eaves Detail, CPR Penticton.
99. PGER Shalalth, B.C. (1941). Track Elevation.
100. Field, British Columbia (1951). Canadian Pacific Railway.
101. CPR's Palliser Square (at centre) Calgary, built 1966-69. *Photo Canadian Pacific.*
102. Canadian National Railways' Churchill, Manitoba (1943). *Provincial Archives of Manitoba.*
103. CNR Saskatoon, Saskatchewan (1964).
104. Waiting Room, CNR Saskatoon (1964).
105. CN Tower, Edmonton, Alberta (1966) by Abugov & Sunderland.
106. Floor Plan of CNR Edmonton Station (1966).
107. CNR Houston, B.C. (1970). Track and End Elevations.
108. PGER North Vancouver Terminal (1956) by Hale & Harrison.
109. Floor Plan, PGER North Vancouver Terminal. *Drawing Courtesy R. F. Harrison.*
110. Edmonton Terminal (1966) of the Northern Alberta Railways.
111. A Typical Small Railway Station Office in Western Canada.
112. CNR Shelter at Innisfree, Alberta, replacement for a Standard Canadian Northern 3rd Class Depot of 1906.

Note: Illustrations without specific credit are the author's. Floor plans redrawn, with permission, from official railway blueprints.

PART ONE

1875-1900

Fig. 1   Meeting the Train, Medicine Hat, Alberta, c.1890.

CENTRUM

The railway station almost inevitably constituted the seed, and eventually the heart of every western Canadian town. It formed the physical core around which business huddled, and from it settlement spread outward, often along Railway Street, which paralleled the tracks. It was the place where nearly all goods and news were received or dispatched, and until about 1940 was without question a community's major link with the outside world.

In early days, a train arrival represented one of the most exciting spectacles in the region, and it seldom failed to attract a sizeable audience of all ages (Fig. 1). Townsfolk commonly gathered in the evening around the waiting room stove to chat, and there was little hesitation to use the station facilities for religious services on Sundays until a regular church could be financed and built.[1] Coupled with memories of special arrivals and departures, these habits and circumstances brought forth an institution undeniably central to the lives and sentiments of virtually all westerners for well over half a century.

Along the new railway lines across the prairies, it was not necessary to have a settlement in order to have a station planned. Long, narrow strips of land unimpeded by level crossings were automatically set aside for depots at six to ten mile intervals. This policy can be traced to Sandford Fleming's 1877 report to Canada's parliament. Fleming (1827-1915) now perhaps best known for his accepted system of world time, was chief civil engineer for the Canadian Pacific Railway in its generative years. His planning for the CPR through the mountains was not complete and perhaps in consequence towns there arose much less systematically than on the prairies. Also, of course, were geographic factors that not only determined routes and available farmland, but level ground safe from avalanches, necessitating much more complex planning and development.

Fleming's standard town plan, which proposed a double lozenge grid of roads around a centralized railway station (Fig. 2) did not become a reality, but the obvious intention of making the station the focal point of the community was largely carried out through other patterns. The commonest one employed can be seen in Figure 3a (Moose Jaw, Sask.). Into this category fall CPR Regina, Calgary and Vancouver, CNR Winnipeg and Edmonton, plus numberless smaller depots. The more rare, double-ended scheme at Beiseker (Fig. 3b) was seldom possible, or for that matter desirable. A union station was a preferred solution, for it reduced costs, land consumption, and the number of level crossings, A variation of the double-end scheme was used in Saskatoon by the Canadian Northern in which the station at one end of the

3

street was matched by the railway's Bessborough Hotel abutting the other. In all cases, it can be seen that a large proportion of a town's traffic was perforce directed towards the railway station, whose silhouette at the end of the main street signalled architectural dominance of the community (a position, incidentally, much coveted by institutions of church and state elsewhere in the world).

Most early stations were simply situated in a manner most convenient for access from the town, but one railway, the Grand Trunk Pacific, consciously sought to take advantage of the winter sun, or so it would appear, by setting stations on the North side of the tracks. The south-facing office and waiting rooms thus received maximum solar exposure and light in cold, dark winter months, and snow and ice on the platforms fronting the depots would tend to disappear a little more quickly. In summer, overheating was avoided by the shade provided by the large overhang of the roof, the sun then being higher in the sky.

Where federal or provincial government land grants were not already made, the increase in overall land values brought about by the coming of a railway was usually sufficient inducement for station grounds to be donated by the communities to be served. But in cases such as Calgary's, where speculators greedily tried to corner the real estate most likely to be used by the CPR, a bitter lesson was taught. The tracks were laid and a station built on inexpensive land further away, and the town was obliged to move to obtain a convenient proximity. Calgary's buildings had to be dragged across the frozen Bow River the following winter, at no small discomfort to the town's contrite inhabitants.

In general, railway stations were not allowed to be built on land set aside as Indian reserve. A three-mile separation between town and reserve was standard policy demanded by government. Every rule must have its exception, however, and Kamsack, Saskatchewan was one example. Indians there wanted a depot, and were in fact successful in the bargain to sell the Canadian Northern Railway some land for a station at ten dollars an acre (not bad for the times).[2]

Townsites on most railways were merely numbered at first. Medicine Hat, for example, was Siding One in its CPR subdivision, Calgary "Siding Twenty". Proper, permanent names soon had to be found, quickly and in abundance, and this resulted in some peculiar practices. Officials naturally enough felt their own names admirably suitable for immortalization on maps and timetables. Donald, in British Columbia, thus derived from Donald Smith of the CPR, one of dozens of such instances. Occasionally, noble efforts of another order were rewarded: the villages of Heskith, Kirkpatrick, Gascoigne, Thrasher and Unwin were named for Canadian Pacific employees decorated for service in the war of 1914-18. On the Northern Alberta

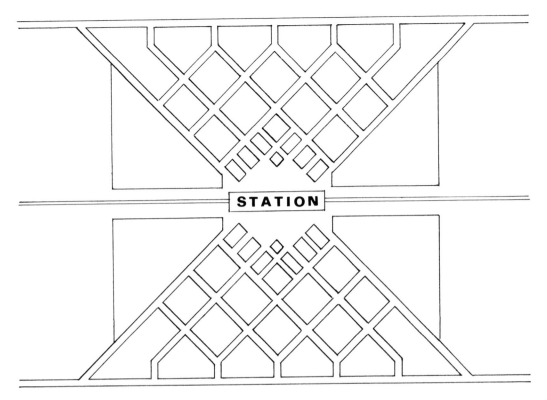

Fig. 2   Sandford Fleming's Proposed Standard Town Plan (1877).

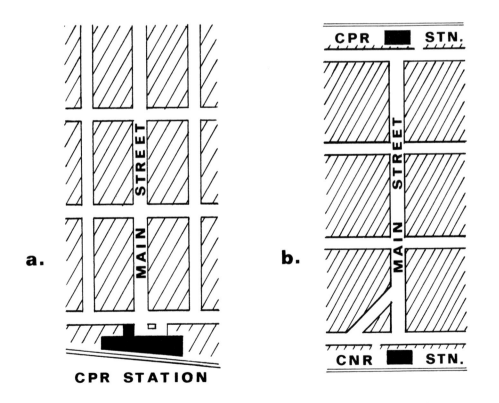

Fig. 3   Common Site Patterns: a) Moose Jaw, Sask. b) Beiseker, Alta.

Railway, it sufficed to be an engineer or conductor to be geographically enshrined, Faust and Culp being two such cases. The most outlandish naming perhaps, was Codesa, made by combining the first two letters of NAR Assistant General Manager Collins, Superintendent Deakin, and Chief Dispatcher Saunders. Only slightly less atrocious was the Grand Trunk Pacific's arrangement of depot names (based upon those of people, or even pets) in alphabetical order along the mainline. Hawkins, Irma, Jarrow and Kinsella, in eastern Alberta, are a reminder of this somewhat desperate solution.

While many stations do continue to operate, countless closures, sales of land (CNR Edmonton and Edson) and moves to peripheral locations (CNR Saskatoon, Brandon, etc.) indicate clearly that the age of the depot as physical centrum is rapidly drawing to a close in western Canada. Socially, the depots seldom attract much attention to-day, although it must be admitted that new uses such as senior citizens' drop-in centres (e.g. Vegreville, Alta.) or restaurants (Vernon, B.C., etc.) do draw numbers of people. But as elsewhere in North America, the growth of alternative modes of transport and communication has reduced the overall importance of railway stations, and it is not likely that they will ever again attain their former prime position in the towns they served so well.

THE FIRST WAVE

While the 1870s saw route surveying activity, and the construction of a short connecting line from St. Boniface, Manitoba to the United States border (of which very little has been recorded regarding railway stations) the story of station building in the Canadian West can be seen to properly begin in the next decade, with the commencement in February, 1881 of the prairie section of the Canadian Pacific Railway.

Because of the temporary nature of initial CPR stations, their design was far from ornate. They were in fact little more than boxcars without wheels, and even Calgary, which already had a small population, received this type (Fig. 4) for a start. The primitive depot's interior contained a tiny bedroom for the agent at one end, a rudimentary office at the other, with a small waiting space containing a bench and stove situated between. Outside, a short wooden platform kept one's feet out of the ubiquitous mud. A second truckless boxcar served for baggage and freight storage, and no foundations were laid for either building, so that removal would be quick and easy when a regular station house was constructed. This Spartan installation was crude, yet baronial in comparison with the Canadian Northern's practice later of using tents as a start, leaving the station operator to set up his telegraph key on a packing case for an interim period.

The commonest CPR station of the 1880s was of the type seen in Figure 5 (Gleichen, Alta.). Its use was not limited to the West (one example in fact still survives at Claremont, in eastern Ontario) but it was repeated again and again across the prairies and down to the Pacific coast, both as shown and in reverse configuration, i.e. with freight shed to the right, doors and windows relocated accordingly. Combination stations such as these, with freight and passenger facilities joined, were considered the most practical for small towns, where the agent was likely to carry out all or most operations. A waiting room, office, and freight room were laid out side by side in that order on the main floor. In this particular model, living quarters for the agent and his family were all located upstairs, but variations developed later, as we shall see in due course.

Closely related was the special station with separate ladies' waiting room built at Medicine Hat (Figs. 1 and 6) where trains halted a half hour for servicing, and where a Mounted Police barracks, several nearby mines, and other commercial activity meant greater than average crowds. The exterior architectural elements were identical to the above type. A skimpy canopy was placed over each window and door on the ground floor, to protect those

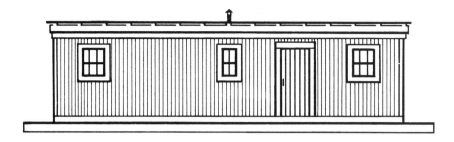
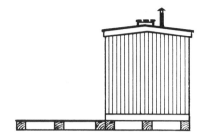

Fig. 4   Portable CPR Station of the 1880s. Track and End Elevations.

Fig. 5   Standard Canadian Pacific Railway Station at Gleichen, Alta.

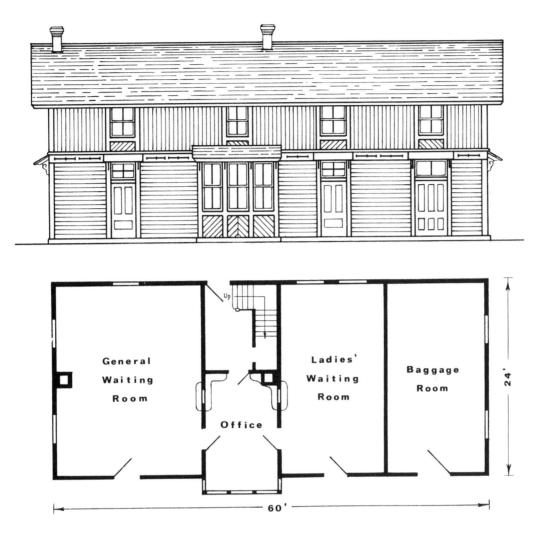

Fig. 6   CPR Medicine Hat (1883). Track Elevation & Ground Floor Plan.

portions of the building from rain and snow. Passengers were expected to endure the weather, or stay inside the station until the last minute. The protruding telegraph bay, which became a feature of nearly all North American railway stations after 1880, was a functional feature that allowed the operator to survey both tracks and surroundings with comparative ease, improving efficiency and security. Decoration was relatively slight. Swiss chalet gable ends, so popular in house design of the late nineteenth century, gave a certain picturesqueness, which was further enhanced by the patterned band between the storeys, spindle finials on the roof peaks, and diagonal sheathing in panels beneath the windows.

Perhaps the most picturesque touch to early CPR stations on the prairies was environmental rather than strictly architectural. It was the presence on the platforms of costumed Indians proffering buffalo horns and other curios to passing tourists. The denizens of the plains were also attracted to the depots by a market for buffalo bones, which often accumulated in vast white piles in the yards, awaiting shipment to eastern sugar refiners, handle markers, and fertilizer companies.[3]

While on the subject of station surroundings, it should be mentioned that vegetable gardens became a common feature almost from the beginning, for imported produce was virtually nonexistant. Lawns and flower beds appeared later, especially after 1902, when seeds and growing information began to be distributed by the railway companies to their agents, and annual competitions were held for the further encouragement of pleasing facilities. Both station gardens and the spelling out of station names in whitewashed stones were English habits of long standing,[4] so that homesick immigrants were contented as much as passing tourists. In the 1890s, bandstands could be found in some station plots (for example Olds, and Calgary, in Alberta) but grounds were generally fenced shut to alleviate upkeep, which was one more task for the already busy agent.

During the first decade of rail service the thinness of population, the great construction expenditures for track, buildings and equipment, and the lack of any significant competition combined to preclude expensive stations anywhere in the West. Apart from the basic string of small, wooden, somewhat standardized depots, only two brick stations and a couple of log structures stand out.

The first brick station was at Winnipeg. The Pembina Branch Railway (a part of the CPR) was completed in December, 1878, linking Manitoba to American rail systems at Crookston, Minnesota. But it was not until 1882, after four long years of hiking to St. Boniface to board trains, that citizens of Winnipeg could finally have the convenience of service within their own town. Opening of the first major terminal in the Canadian West had been delayed by the lack of a railway bridge across the Red River.

Though not ornate, the sturdy-looking yellow brick Winnipeg terminal did manage to hint discretely at ancestral roots in both the classical world and the Middle Ages (Fig. 7). Roman arches in grey stone decorated the end walls, and a medieval, partial-hipped bay projected from midway along the upper track facade. To provide a modish touch, the station's dining room featured wicker furniture, and polished silverware on sparkling white linen reminded the visitor that while the plains still remained to be fully tamed, the city could offer all the niceties of the East. Another urbane feature of the building was to have been a trackside canopy, which plans reveal was intended at least, but which it appears was never attained. Perhaps the company was too preoccupied with its other works, or its land sales, many of which were made from offices in this very building.

Fig. 7   First CPR Station at Winnipeg, Manitoba (1882).

Fig. 8   CPR Log Station at Laggan, Alberta (1886).

Fig. 9   Rogers' Pass, British Columbia. Selkirk Mountain Range.

Fig. 10   CPR Glacier House, British Columbia (1886).

Brandon, the second most important centre in early Manitoba, saw Canadian Pacific service begin in September, 1881. The first Brandon station was similar in style and materails to the Winnipeg terminal, but was of two storeys only in the centre third of its length. The depot was replaced in 1911 by the more elaborate building described in Part Two.

Of particular interest along the CPR line in the Rockies, were the 1886 log stations at Laggan (Fig. 8) and Banff. Special designs were made for these two vacation resorts in an effort to create an appropriate air of cosiness and closeness to nature. Round, peeled logs formed the walls, and slender poles were employed for canopy brackets and station name lettering. To add grace, or perhaps a reminder of home to visitors from the city, the woodsy structures were capped (not a little incongruously) with concave mansard roofs. The Banff log depot no longer exists, but the Laggan station still stood as of this writing, serving as an elegant storage shed for oil drums, track spikes, and other railway materials. A few dozen yards away, the larger log station, of 1909, catered to passengers under the name given the stop during World War I, Lake Louise.

A hundred miles west of this point by rail lay the greatest obstacle faced by the CPR, the Selkirk range of mountains (Fig. 9). It was only in 1883, at the last conceivable moment, that a pass through this very formidable barrier was found by a wiry American surveyor for the railway, Major A. B. Rogers. Grades to its 4300 foot summit were exceedingly steep, however, and the small locomotives of the period required the elimination of dining cars from their trains in order to sufficiently lighten the load. Consequently, a lunch stop was made at the top of the pass. The hotel where meals were served can be seen behind the tiny Glacier station shown in Figure 10. Guide books of the period suggested that one stroll after dinner to the Great Glacier, a little over a mile away. Construction of the Connaught Tunnel brought about the abandonment of the dangerous pass route around 1916, ending the usefulness of the depot and its hotel. A larger station, of logs and similar in style to the second Laggan depot perpetuated the name "Glacier" at a point further down the valley, but the original stop is now only a part of history.

A final note concerns the first western terminus of the CPR, built beside the wharf at Port Moody, B.C. in 1886. It was a fairly small, gambrel-roofed, two-storey frame building, whose architecture was of no particular merit, but whose mention historically can not in fairness be overlooked.[5]

THE GRAND MANNER

On the North American continent generally, the late nineteenth century was an age of lavishness. Pullman cars were mobile palaces, and plush mansions, Grand Hotels, and extravagant railway terminals were commonplace. It was not surprising, therefore, that the trappings of opulence arrived in the sparsely-settled Canadian West by the mid-1890s, and began to impose an air of stability, if not splendour on a land so recently wilderness.

The Canadian Pacific dominated the railway scene in western Canada to the end of the century, encountering no significant competition. A small independent railway, the Manitoba & North Western was built in 1886 from Portage la Prairie to Minnedosa, but any threat it might have posed to the giant CPR ended in May 1900, when it was leased to that company for the following 999 years. An American railway, the Northern Pacific, encroached on CPR territory in southern Manitoba in 1888, but although it gained ground in its early years the NPR remained relatively unimportant so far as Canada was concerned.

The Northern Pacific's tiny, typically American single-storey wooden depots were of little architectural consequence, but not so was the grandiose station-hotel built in Winnipeg and opened on New Year's Day, 1892. The seven-storey edifice (Fig. 11) situated at Main and Water Streets was the first of the chateau style in the Canadian West, and preceded the CPR's Chateau Frontenac at Quebec by several months.[6] There can be little doubt that directly influencing both projects was Theodore Link's well publicized Union Station in St. Louis (1891-94) a huge terminal related in forms to the late medieval chateaux of France. Over the nexty forty-five years Canada adopted the style nationally, using it for both railway and government buildings on a grand scale.

Architect for the Northern Pacific's Manitoba Hotel and station was C. E. Joy, of St. Paul Minnesota. Joy designed the hotel as a hollow triangle to fit the site, and placed a low station with train shed at the back. A base of red stone, walls of pressed brick, and a shingled attic combined in what was considered the finest hotel and station west of Montreal. As one of Winnipeg's best buildings, it posed a challenge to CPR leadership, but the problem was resolved one bitterly cold night in February 1899, when fire reduced all but the train shed to ashes. This misfortune, coupled with a temporary bankruptcy five years earlier, undermined the railway company's ability to continue operations in Manitoba. Soon afterward, the lines were leased to the provincial government, and in January 1901 their control passed to the Canadian Northern Railway.

Fig. 11   Northern Pacific Railway's Winnipeg Station-Hotel (1892).

Fig. 12   Canadian Pacific Railway Station at Regina, Sask. (1892).

Fig. 13   Second CPR Calgary Station (1893).

The Canadian Pacific, no doubt realizing it would eventually have to face strong competition, began to build several excellent stations in the 1890s to fortify its premier position in the West. Regina received the first of the improved depots in 1892. The towered brick edifice (Fig. 12) was in part a compensation to the Queen City for diversion of eastbound traffic over the new Soo Line that ran south from Moose Jaw, a development not at all to the liking of Regina merchants.

The Regina station, by Edward Colonna[7] featured an exterior of red brick on a grey stone base, and a broad, flaring hipped roof whose overhang provided generous protection against both storm and soot. It is not known whether this was the first time that this general design was used on the CPR, but it became a common company style for many years following.

Calgary got a fine new sandstone station (Fig. 13) in 1893. No tower was incorporated into the design, but a separate dining building (connected by covered passageway) must have made up for any slight Calgarians might have felt. Lawns, flower beds, a fountain and bandstand composed a pleasant setting. When demolition took place in 1911, to make way for the Palliser Hotel, a somewhat vicarious survival was achieved for the station through the careful dismantling of its stone for reuse in depots at High River and Claresholm a few miles to the South.

As the century drew to a close, the Canadian Pacific built four particularly impressive stations in the West, all of them designed by Montreal architect Edward Maxwell.[8] Foremost of this group was the Vancouver terminal (Fig. 14) opened in 1898.

The future city of Vancouver was still virgin forest when the CPR was built, and it was not until 1887 that train service began to a humble wooden depot named "Hastings" near what is now the downtown area.[9] Population was only in the hundreds at that time, yet only a decade passed before the seaport and traffic had grown to a point where one of the finest railway terminals in Canada was begun, at a site at the foot of Granville Street.

The robust new station rose eight full storeys in the centre block, and four in the wings. Seen from the South, i.e. from Cordova Street, two storeys were hidden, for the tracks at the back of the station were at a lower level. On the street facade, two powerful towers, one round the other polygonal, supported a low and massive 42 foot arch over the main entrance. Rough-faced Calgary stone was employed there and around the base, but special moisture-resistant buff brick was brought from Victoria for the rest of the wall construction. Slate roofs with copper-capped ridges and dormers further added to the durability of the structure, but all was somewhat in vain, for the bold chateau of no mean architectural beauty lasted only until 1914.

On the main floor, level with the street, the ticket office was found in the middle of the general waiting room, an idea rarely used again until the

17

Fig. 14   CPR Vancouver Terminal (1898) by Edward Maxwell.

Fig. 15   CPR Station-Hotel at Moose Jaw, Sask. (1898) by E. Maxwell.

18

Ottawa Union, and the CNR Edmonton terminals were built in 1966. As was customary in the larger stations, a separate women's waiting room was provided, and stairs and elevators connected these areas with a reception and departure hall below, at track level. Baggage and express were, of course, also handled on the ground floor in proximity of the tracks. Upper floors of the station were devoted to railway office space.

Maxwell's second CPR masterpiece in the West was a combined station and hotel for Moose Jaw (Fig. 15). Like Vancouver II, it was begun in 1898, and once again Calgary stone harmonized with Victoria brick. The 200 by 34 foot edifice contained a dining room, thirty bedrooms with bath, and all normal station facilities. Other features were a central passageway leading from street to tracks, and a second floor bay window for the station operator.

While the Moose Jaw project was under construction, yet a third Maxwell station was commenced at Sicamous, British Columbia (Fig. 16). As early as 1888 a railway hotel had been planned for the scenic lakeside location. Bruce Price, a Boston architect employed by the CPR for its first major buildings — Windsor Station in Montreal amongst others — had drawn plans, but they got no further.[10] After track was laid in 1891 from Sicamous to Okanagan Landing, where lakeboats completed access to Penticton, a better station also seemed required. But it was not until fire destroyed the original tiny depot in 1897, that impetus was finally given for construction of the much-needed station and hotel, which were combined under one roof.

The new Sicamous building featured a central pavilion with polygonal turrets, but similarity to Moose Jaw station-hotel ended there. Shingled walls, leaded glass windows, balconies, and fantastic hooked gable ends produced a decidedly rustic effect. An extension in 1910 added 25 more bedrooms to the hotel's original 28, demonstrating the success of the venture, and patronage was steady until the late 1950s, when train service into the Okanagan was eliminated, and trains on the mainline reduced. Closure and demolition of the station-hotel was then both inevitable and swift.

Completing the Maxwell quartet of western stations was the 90 by 40 foot brick and stone depot at New Westminster, B.C. (Fig. 17). Although this was the smallest of the four stations (and incidentally the only one to survive to the present) it nonetheless achieved a striking monumentality. The two massive towers on the track side, and the bold yet ornate masonry all round imparted an unequivocal impression of eternal solidity and importance (Fig. 18). Changes to the exterior have been slight since construction in 1899, but the renovations necessary to convert the building to use as a restaurant and lounge in recent years left little of the interior untouched. A ticket office remains in the former baggage room, but the proud old station is now merely a grand spectator to the trains that pass but no longer stop.

Fig. 16   Maxwell's CPR Station-Hotel for Sicamous, B.C. (1898).

Fig. 17   Canadian Pacific's New Westminster, B.C. (1899) by E. Maxwell.

20

Fig. 18   Detail of Masonry, CPR New Westminster, B.C. (1899).

MINOR STATIONS OF THE 1890s

Minor stations were in all cases of the one-side variety, i.e. with the house set to one side of the tracks, and fronted by a wooden platform between eight and sixteen feet in width. Waiting rooms were arranged to open directly onto the platform for minimum confusion and delay when trains arrived, and the office of the agent was strategically placed between freight and passenger facilities in virtually every instance. Neatness and operating economy were governing principles, but moldings and scrollsaw work could appear on even the most minor of stations. A few of the best examples of small 1890 depots are examined below.

The CPR Vancouver engineering office was responsible for the design of gambrel-roofed Agassiz (Fig. 19). Good headroom was possible upstairs with this style of roof, but it was not commonly used, perhaps because of the added number of cubic feet to be enclosed and heated. Scrollsawn window sash (Fig. 20) originally ornamented the building, and fish scale pattern shingles gave vitality to the gables. Sheathing was of wooden drop siding (Fig. 21) the favorite material of the period. Like so many old CPR stations, Agassiz was insul-bricked in the late 1940s or early 50s. This fibreboard covering, coated with asphalt and tiny colored stones arranged to imitate brick was an economical solution to the need for insulation and reduced maintenance costs as stations weathered and fuel prices rose.

The picturesque depot for Virden, Manitoba (Figs. 22 and 23) was a product of R. B. Pratt.[11] Of particular interest are the unusual vee-shaped telegraph bay, the curved, bonnet-like roofs, beaked gables, and the solid stone walls 18 inches thick. Cozy fireplaces in the waiting rooms indicate special status for the station, for such amenities were not at all common. Because construction of this 1899 station was delayed until 1906, another bizarre feature was added as well. Pratt had left the CPR to work for the Canadian Northern in the intervening period, resulting in the two competing railways building stations in the same town at almost the same time, using plans (not the same ones of course, the CNR was a special variant of the 3rd Class standard) by the same architect.

When a station design proved to be particularly pleasing, it was not uncommon for the railway companies to try to make use of it again, either as a base for a standard plan, or for another special. In the case of Canadian Pacific's Virden, a similar depot was built about the same time at Morden, Manitoba. Roofs, dormers and general shapes were almost identical. Room layout differed somewhat (apparently a reverse configuration) but there were

Fig. 19   CPR Agassiz, B.C. (1893) as it appeared in the 1970s.

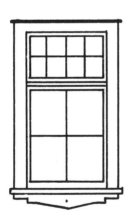

Fig. 20   Original Window Sash, CPR Agassiz.

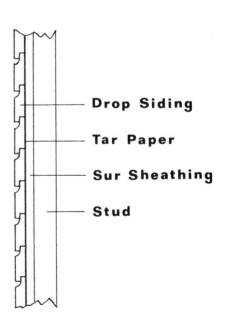

Drop Siding

Tar Paper

Sur Sheathing

Stud

Fig. 21   Cross Section of a Wall with Drop Siding.

23

Fig. 22   CPR Virden, Manitoba (1899) by R. B. Pratt. Built 1906.

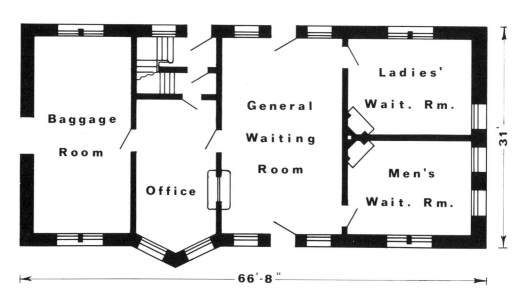

Fig. 23   Ground Floor Plan, CPR Virden, Manitoba (1899).

24

no major differences between the two stations apart from the use of frame construction for Morden, as opposed to stone for Virden.

Any place designated by name in the railway timetable is a station on Canadian railways, hence shelters deserve some mention. There are no office or living quarters in shelters, for traffic does not warrant an agent. Furniture is usually limited to a bench and a stove, although a counter for writing may sometimes also be found. Moberly (Fig. 24) is a fine example of the shelters built in the 1890s, for its thorough construction and touch of imagination are typical for the period. Interior walls of the waiting room were completely sheathed with vee-groove lumber, and the under eaves fully enclosed. The partial-hipped, or jerkin-head roof was a fancy touch not repeated on shelters after the turn of the century. Twentieth-century Canada tended to be much more sobre (compare Fig. 112).

Fig. 24   CPR Shelter at Moberly, British Columbia (c. 1893).

Though not abundant in western Canada until after the turn of the century, some very important branch lines were built shortly before. Stations along these lines, which were generally begun by small companies were quite distinctive in style, and the following survey will attempt to cover the highlights.

The Calgary & Edmonton Railway, first leased then bought by the CPR, was built in 1891 from Macleod (near Lethbridge) to Strathcona (South Edmonton). The Innisfail station (Fig. 25) illustrates the standard C&ER depot, which one notices had a partial hip only on the roof end facing the tracks. This feature appears to be a touch of Victorian whimsy, carried out for picturesque rather than any practical reasons. Roof overhangs were skimpy, adding to the domestic character of the depot. To the right of the station can be seen the typical Canadian hexagonal enclosed water tower that was found along all but Pacific coast lines after Canadian Pacific's development of the design around the turn of the century. The lower enclosure contained a pump boiler, to prevent freezing of the tank's water in winter. An earlier, cylindrical enclosed tower may be seen in Figures 9 and 16.

Resembling the stations of the C&ER were those built a few months earlier for the Qu'Appelle, Long Lake & Saskatchewan Railway. The first depot in Saskatoon was of this type.[12] The Canadian Pacific's involvement with both lines (the CPR leased the QALL&SR from 1890 to 1906) and the use of the same contractors, Mackenzie & Mann, very probably accounts for the similarity of the two lines' stations.

In the Okanagan valley, meanwhile, the Shuswap & Okanagan Railway was also under construction. As indicated earlier, the CPR mainline was connected from Sicamous to Okanagan Landing in 1891. Stations of the S&OR were much more varied in style than those of either of the two branch lines mentioned above. The first Vernon station was a standard CPR design of a type used on the mainline in the region, but the Enderby depot was in fact a converted hotel, and Armstrong, the only other important town on the line was given the unique depot shown in figure 26. The Armstrong station, somewhat the worse for wear and insul-bricking, now lacks eaves brackets, but the outstanding architectural feature present from the beginning has been left intact: the diagonally set window in the attic. The abberation was probably an on-the-spot builder's solution to the problem of a high adjoining freight shed.

The closing years of the century saw the CPR undertake a vital branch line from Lethbridge, in southern Alberta, to Kootenay Landing in southeastern British Columbia. This line, known as the Crow's Nest Branch Railway, after the mountain pass on its route, had stations of different design than those of the parent company. The standard Second Class station house

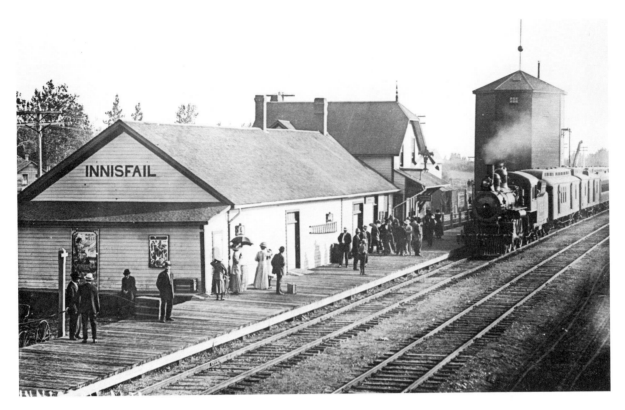

Fig. 25   Innisfail, Alberta. Calgary & Edmonton Railway (1891).

Fig. 26   Shuswap & Okanagan (CPR) Station at Armstrong, B.C. (1892).

Fig. 27   CPR Crow's Nest Branch Standard 2nd Class Station (1898).

(Fig. 27) was given a very dominant A-shaped dormer on the track elevation, and the extremely steep roof, with eight-foot overhangs at front and sides (though not at the back) was another important feature. One example of the Second Class type survived at Elko in 1975, and the First Class wooden depot at Fernie also persisted, but most of the remainder have disappeared since cessation of passenger service at the end of the 1950s.

From the foregoing chapters it should be apparent that although the number of railways in western Canada was relatively small before 1900, variety and quality in stations was not lacking. And while much was owed to architectural design elsewhere, one can nevertheless detect a regional distinctness through the absence of any strongly Gothic features so common in eastern stations, and the total avoidance of Spanish Mission styling much favoured in the American south and west. It is unfortunate that expansion after the turn of the century brought about the eventual destruction of most of the finer examples from the early years, but we can take some comfort from the fact that these accomplishments of the era did survive to a certain degree in photographic form.

PART TWO

1900 - 1940

INTRODUCTORY HISTORY

The end of the Canadian Pacific's virtual monopoly in the western provinces at the turn of the century set the stage for an era of station building even more vigorous and varied than before. Important rival railways developed which at first chose to serve areas to the north of the CPR lines. Then, as branches began to run south into CP territory, the Canadian Pacific responded by extending its Manitoba & Northwestern Railway from Yorkton through Saskatoon to Wetaskiwin, just south of Edmonton. The architectural offices of all companies hummed with activity as the necessary multitude of new stations was draughted.

The Canadian Northern Railway, formed in 1898, was the first of the major new companies. It began as a short line in Manitoba, running from Gladstone to Dauphin, but very soon Winnipeg was linked and the lakehead connected. Expansion northwesterly, into the rich farmland surrounding the original route proposed and surveyed by Sandford Fleming for the CPR followed. By 1915, the fledgling Canadian Northern had breached the Yellowhead Pass, laid rails to Vancouver in the West, Montreal in the East, and constructed an enormous network of branches over the prairies. Left to develop its enterprise, the new transcontinental would probably have survived the financial stresses of the 1914-18 war.

Unfortunately, the Laurier government in Ottawa decided to back a third major railway venture into the West, in the process straining the credit market severely, and slicing the traffic pie into morsels too small to properly sustain any of the companies. The federal government's agreement with the Grand Trunk Railway in 1903 brought about the formation of the Grand Trunk Pacific. A government-financed National Transcontinental connection between Quebec and Winnipeg was built, and official opening of the new GTPR took place in April, 1914.

In spite of the development of hardier strains of wheat that made northern farming possible, and strenuous efforts by government to populate the areas served by the new railways, financial troubles loomed ominously before the war. By 1920, the CNR and the GTPR were obliged to merge with the government's Intercolonial Railway, to form Canadian National Railways. The venerable Grand Trunk, itself victim of political and managerial bungling, became part of the new system two years later.

It is useful to note that the Grand Trunk Pacific did not develop a very extensive branchline network in the West. Indeed, in Manitoba there were no branches at all, for competitors had already blanketed most of the prosperous farm areas. Despite the GTPR's monopoly of the area northwest of the Yellowhead, all the way to terminus at Prince Rupert, that isolated mountain region too proved nearly impossible to branch in, for settlement was difficult and railway building extra costly. The total number of GTPR stations was thus small in comparison with either the Canadian Northern or the CPR.

Although competition continued to be keen in the new century, tempers were generally kept in check. Confrontations between rivals did not reach the pitch of the Great Northern — Canadian Pacific battle of the 1890s in southern British Columbia, which saw a GNR crew attack the CPR's new Sandon station by night, demolish the freight shed and using chain and locomotive tow the little depot to the nearest creek.

Architecturally, the new railways followed the precedents set by the CPR in regard to small stations. Because living accommodations were generally difficult to find, they were provided on the premises for the Agent and his family (unlike the U.S.A., where it was the exception rather than the rule). Wooden, standardized depots were chosen by all the railways for most points in order to economize on material costs as well as construction time, and by building large dormers, otherwise unusable attics became comfortable bedroom space. Stucco exteriors came into widespread use by the end of the 1920s, particularly on the Canadian National Railways. This and other stylistic developments will be examined in the following chapters.

Fig. 28   Winnipeg CPR II (1904) by W.S. and E. Maxwell.

MANITOBA CLASSICS

As early as 1899 the Canadian Pacific was planning a new, larger Winnipeg station. The design first considered was of French chateau style, with a great round tower facing the corner of Main and Higgins Streets.[13] It was expected that work would commence the following year, but problems of land acquisition for an accompanying hotel and underpass caused delay of construction until June, 1904. By that date, a completely different design was decided upon, one of Roman classical style. Neo-Roman splendour at the Chicago Columbian Exposition of 1893 had thereafter heavily influenced commercial architecture, and it was also at this time that classic-biased Parisian Beaux Arts training gained considerable favor amongst North American architects.

Great columns and arches were eminently suited to the needs of railway architecture of the time, for not only were security and strength implied but wide openings for entrances, and airy, unobstructed interior spaces easily created. It should be pointed out, however, that most arches and vaults used in twentieth century Roman style buildings were solely for decorative effect and historic association with power and empire. The development of reliable steel girders already allowed great and economical spanning, and indeed it can be observed that the majority of ceilings, though sometimes enormous, were built flat.

The firm of W.S. and E. Maxwell was engaged as architects for Winnipeg CPR II (Fig. 28) and it is thus to them that credit must go for the first classical terminal in the Canadian West. The Beaux Arts training of the younger Maxwell (later architect for the Saskatchewan legislative building) is particularly apparent in the meticulous, ornate facade, and it would appear that he was responsible for most of the project, which is decidedly different in character from the massive earlier CPR stations designed by Edward.[14]

The companion Royal Alexandra Hotel, and the connecting corridor building that contained a baggage room no longer stand, but the grey stone/red brick station is essentially intact as of this writing. The monumental portico, 55 feet wide and 40 feet high contains two pairs of huge stone columns resting on great pedastels that dwarf, almost intimidate passersby. Richly carved garlands and horns of plenty enhance a central clock overhead. Fortunately, through all the changes over the years the street facade of Winnipeg II remained untouched, and can thus be counted to-day as a monument to an era of glorious railway architecture.

It is difficult now to form a fair opinion of the interior, for rich green walls, dark-stained oak woodwork, and golden-toned glazes on capitals and friezes have succumbed to the effects of pastel paints. All dignity has perished. Extensive structural alterations in 1915 changed some of the interior, and much of the rear exterior where tracks were raised six feet to allow an underground midway with more baggage room.

Canadian Pacific's magnificence did not remain long without challenge in Winnipeg. The Union Station (Fig. 29) built to serve patrons of Canadian Northern and Grand Trunk Pacific, opened its doors in August, 1911. For this unusually large and competitively strategic terminal, the New York architectural firm of Warren & Wetmore was engaged. Its reputation was currently aglow through association with the design of Grand Central station in New York, one of the finest in the United States.

The handsome triumphal arch motif for the front entrance of Winnipeg Union Station can be traced as far back in railway architecture as Philip Hardwick's famous arch at Euston, in London (1835) but the highly ornamental Art Nouveau canopy over the restaurant entrance to the left (Fig. 30) was a contemporary touch.

The domed, circular lobby 88 feet in diameter and lying directly behind the entrance arch, constituted the major internal feature. Like most other giant terminals of its day, there was no seating or obstruction of any kind in this huge area so as not to impede traffic to and from trains. Waiting rooms and restaurant were placed in the north wing, tickets and baggage in the south. Offices of the railways were located in the upper floors, arranged in open courts so that natural daylight could enter both the offices and the skylights over the waiting and ticket areas (Fig. 31).

When built, the basement of the north wing was devoted to immigrants, who at that time were arriving in train loads. Special waiting, lunch, laundry and bath rooms were provided, a welcome convenience for the largely non-English speaking people fresh off the ships from Europe a mere week before.

The optimism of the railways was reflected in the station's construction and generous size. Steelwork and foundations were designed to allow another five floors. Concrete train platforms twenty feet wide could handle up to two hundred large passenger coaches at any one time. The interior of the lobby and general waiting room were wainscotted with marble to a height of six feet, and terrazzo and iron made the most durable floors and stairs.

Winnipeg Union Station's train shed is of interest not only because it was one of the few in the West, but because it was of the Bush type, an economical substitute for the lofty iron and glass enclosures of the nineteenth century.[15] Open slots above the tracks vented exhaust smoke from the locomotives. The elements were sufficiently excluded, although the atmosphere within the sheds could be rather sombre on dull days.

While the Winnipeg Union terminal was under construction, the city of Brandon received not one but two classical stations. Both Canadian Pacific

Fig. 29   Winnipeg Union Station (1911) by Warren & Wetmore.

Fig. 30   Restaurant Entrance, Winnipeg Union Station (1911).

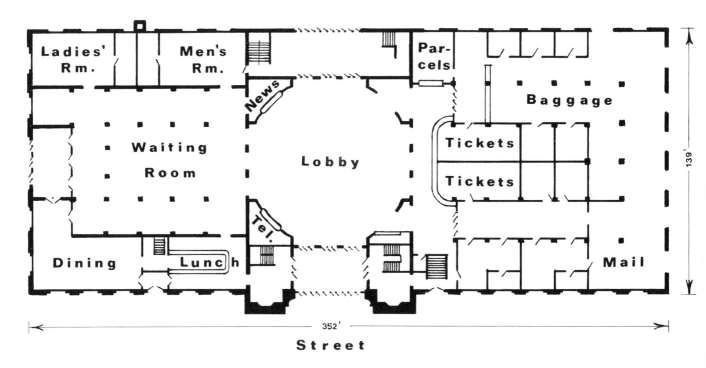

Tracks

Ladies' Rm.

Men's Rm.

Par-cels

News

Baggage

Waiting Room

Lobby

Tickets

Tickets

Tel.

Dining

Lunch

Mail

139'

352'

Street

Fig. 31   Plan of Main Floor, Winnipeg Union Station (1911).

and Canadian Northern built passenger facilities in the growing community in 1911, a big year for station construction in the West generally.

The Canadian Northern's temple to the gods of steam and iron was very restrained (Fig. 32). Two large, pedimented pseudo porches along the lengthy facade suggested grandeur, while an intervening pair of smaller entrance porticos added a touch of grace. Pediment decoration was unpretentious, consisting simply of the company's crest, and the date of the station's construction. Following English practice, the low station was fronted by a tall hotel, the two connected by corridor. The Prince Edward Hotel still operated in the 1970s, but the station had for several years been converted into a pub, and Canadian National's passengers travelled seven miles north of the town to board the few trains that continued to run.

The Canadian Pacific's station (Fig. 33) remained downtown and little changed. Its classicism, highly vigorous and manneristic, elicits groans or applause — depending upon one's artistic creed. Triglyphs not only occupy their normal place in the frieze, they ornament pilaster capitals as well. Heavy keystones embellished with consoles protrude from main floor window frames, while heavily streaked stone shrieks from the balustrade above. A clock completes the fanciful facade's eclectic pediment. Ictinus would surely have moaned, but admirers of Giulio Romano will find the recipe delightful! Classicism on the prairies was in full bloom, and as can be seen by these Manitoba examples, lay in competent and clever hands.

Fig. 32   CNR Brandon, Manitoba (1911), Prince Edward Hotel at right.

Fig. 33   Canadian Pacific's Brandon, Manitoba Station (1911).

COMPETITION'S SPUR

Almost every western Canadian town of reasonable size or importance received at least one new station in the highly competitive years between 1900 and 1920. Some were replacements for earlier, obsolete depots. Many represented the new railways' efforts to gain public attention and confidence.

The Canadian Northern Railway firmly planted its banner in the Northwest with its first Edmonton station (Fig. 34). Trains of an associated short line, the Edmonton, Yukon & Pacific, had been depositing goods and passengers at a plain, wooden depot on the river flats beneath downtown Edmonton since October, 1902. It was therefore a jubilant crowd that gathered in late November, 1905 to witness the silver spike ceremony marking the arrival of the CNR and the opening of its new, castle-like terminal, even if it was not quite finished. This, and the twin-towered Port Arthur (Ontario) station stood at what were then the ends of the system, and were the only sizeable CNR depots until 1910.

Echoes of Edmonton station, with its turreted, cubic central block, flanking lower wings, chateauesque dormers and wide roofs were eventually to be found in other large Canadian Northern depots. Saskatoon (1910) was very similar, differing mainly in its greater length and simpler gabling. The Dauphin, Manitoba station (1912) was another, similar version.

The spur of competition drove all the companies to a feverish pitch of building activity. The Canadian Pacific bolstered its position by constructing a series of new brick stations in 1907 at Saskatoon, South Edmonton, Medicine Hat and Lethbridge. All had short, polygonal towers, and sturdy, grey stone bases. Saskatoon was distinctive for its yellow brick, the rest were of the more usual red. Modifications in subsequent years have quite substantially enlarged these stations. Saskatoon was lengthened in 1918 to unite it with its initially separate express building. Medicine Hat II was twinned, and interlinked by a double-gabled section containing a pair of Palladian windows and herring-bone gable ends (frontispiece page vi). Red Deer (Fig. 35) was of the same family of designs as these depots, but was built about 1910.

Banff CPR II (Fig. 36) was fortunate enough to have a very distinctive design, one that has helped to make it perhaps the most well known of all Canadian stations. Rough-cast stucco was set above uncut stone, and the effect rivaled log structures in rusticity and informality. As with most stations of the period, the platform was of wooden planks, beneath which small boys enjoyed hunting for lost coins.

Fig. 34   Canadian Northern Railway's Edmonton Station (1905).

Fig. 35   Canadian Pacific's Red Deer, Alberta Station (1910).

Fig. 36   CPR's Second Banff Station (1910).

Fig. 37   CPR Wilkie, Saskatchewan (1906-08).

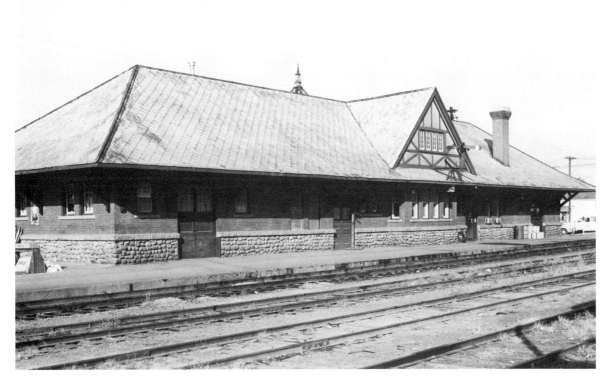

Fig. 38   Canadian Pacific's Vernon, B.C. Station (1911).

Fig. 39   CPR Standard Number Five Station, Bow Island, Alta. (1911).

Among the other visually interesting small CPR stations of the 1900-1920 period was the wooden depot at Wilkie, Saskatchewan (Fig. 37) situated on the second CPR mainline. The Wilkie station has for reasons unknown, a strong Germanic flavour deriving chiefly from the central roof's medieval Rhenish form. This type still survives to-day, incidentally, on old houses and inns in such Teutonic towns as Bacherach-am-Rhein.

Vernon's attractive station (Fig. 38) deserves mention also as one of the more successful of the pre-1914 designs. The heavy cobblestone base, similar to Banff's, had a dual role. It provided rustic charm and at the same time withstood the usual scuffing associated with station activity, without showing the slightest sign of wear. Strictly ornamental are the half-timbered dormer and turret (the latter unfortunately almost hidden in the illustration) which light a completely unfinished attic, to which in fact no stairs lead.

Plain and straightforward almost to a fault was the CPR's Number Five standard station, one of the most common of the period. In Bow Island (Fig. 39) we find a perfect example of this design, built in 1911. Obviously not gorgeous, it could only have been good efficiency and economy that accounted for the design's wide popularity.

Amongst the more important construction of 1910-11 was the large new Calgary station (Fig. 40) the CPR's third in the city in less than thirty years. Local sandstone, though by this time becoming scarce, was employed again, as it had been for the previous depot, of 1893. The new station boasted a low, segmental arch across the main entrance, and the cubic central block likewise seemed to recall the general ideas of Maxwell's CPR Vancouver, of a little over a decade earlier. Different, however, were the accompanying classical pilasters, dentils and consoles that decorated the surfaces. Although not as magnificent as Winnipeg II, it was worthy of royal visits, such as that of King George VI in 1939.

Calgary terminals of the other two major railways could not lay claim to either great size or beauty. The GTP and the Canadian Northern considered constructing a large union depot in the city as late as 1910, but eventually concentrated their capital elsewhere.[16]

The Grand Trunk Pacific opened a temporary station in 1914, but a more permanent building was erected soon afterward on the flats below the former Mounted Police barracks. That depot became part of the freight sheds after amalgamation with the Canadian Northern.

A temporary station also sufficed for the Canadian Northern when it began operating passenger trains into Calgary in 1913. The replacement (Fig. 41) was likewise intended to be temporary, but endured until service to the city ceased in 1971. This station is unique in western Canadian station history, for it was built in 1905 as a parish hall. Then for seven years it was a boys' school, before being purchased by Canadian Northern in 1914. The

Fig. 40   Calgary CPR III (1908) with the Royal Visit of 1939.

Fig. 41   Canadian Northern's Calgary

Terminal (1905-16).

centrally-located, grey stone edifice was renovated relatively little for use as a railway terminal. Most noticeable was the red brick express shed added to the rear. Double doors on the front, and a large electric sign in the pediment to cover the "St. Mary's Hall" inscription were the other main changes. The station was opened for traffic in December, 1916.

Canadian Pacific's management could not have been pleased with their rivals' incursions into Calgary, nor with their success in Edmonton, which the CPR had resolutely resisted serving beyond the south banks of the Saskatchewan River, reached in 1891. The growth of Edmonton went on, however, and when it became the capital of the province of Alberta early in the century, it became obvious that direct access was imperative if the CPR was to compete very effectively in the city. In 1912, therefore, the great High Level Bridge, nearly a half mile long was constructed over the 160 foot deep river valley. A few blocks north of the bridge, at Jasper Avenue, a classical terminal of medium size took form. Attempts at modernization after 1945 removed any elegance the original building once had. Small-paned windows were replaced with large ones, the stone stuccoed over and painted a pinkish beige, and the cornice completely shaved away. Discontinuance of passenger service in 1973 mercifully ended further surgery, although the deserted structure then became a candidate for the wrecker's hammer.

Many cities and towns would have preferred Union Stations to the often widely-spaced independent terminals usually set up by each of the railways. Transfers are avoided, road traffic less interrupted, and valuable space saved with the union terminal system.

When under duress of some sort, the companies would agree to cooperate in use of stations. After 1909, the GTPR used the CNR's Edmonton station but mainly because the Canadian Northern's choice location could not be matched. The same was true in Winnipeg in 1911, when there was a substantial benefit to the CN in the fact that a good connection with the National Transcontinental (GTPR's link with the East) could be made. The GTP resisted in Saskatoon, where a lucrative taxi monopoly served an inconveniently placed station, and in Calgary both railways were unable to come to an agreement on a joint terminal. At Regina, all three major railways eventually ended using the same station (the CPR's) but only after the GTP had tried its own, and the CPR was faced with an arrangement whereby a line it had leased (the QALL&SR) passed to the Canadian Northern Railway and the federal Board of Railway Commissioners insisted that no change of station be made. Canadian Pacific accommodations were exceedingly rare.

It was not until the amalgamation of the CNR and the GTPR in the early 1920s that any great progress toward common use of small stations was made. An exception was the Portage la Prairie union depot (Fig. 42) built in 1908.

In the Portage la Prairie station's appearance one notes the characteristic neatness and avoidance of visible eaves brackets favoured by the GTPR. The half-timbering in the gables denotes English Domestic Revival stylistic influence on station architecture in Canada, after a strong popularity in Britain around the turn of the century. Apart from the fact that two companies were supporting the station, one can surmise that it was stiff competition that produced this better than average small town depot, at a time when passengers (who were obviously potential shippers as well) were often wooed and pampered by the railways.

Fig. 42   Union Station at Portage la Prairie, Manitoba (1908).

VANCOUVER TRIAD

Vancouver probably fared the best of all in the pre-war contests between rail companies. Three costly terminals arose in the coastal city between 1912 and 1919.

First of the Vancouver trio was the CPR's 380 foot-long steel, brick and stone structure (Fig. 43) completed in 1914. The architects, Barrott, Blackader and Webster, of Montreal, arranged the station in a wedge shape so that all available ground space could be utilized. The lobby and general waiting room were placed centrally, behind the street facade's great colonnade, and this area (Fig. 44) being well lit by south-facing windows became one of the sunniest in Canadian terminals. Large models of Canadian Pacific steamships once decorated the room but have long since been removed. What has remained of the original ornamentation is the series of scenic oil paintings in the frieze. They were the work of a local artist, Adelaide Langford,[17] and although not too easily seen at such a height they have provided a measure of enjoyment to waiting passengers over the years. In connection with the station's decor it should also be mentioned that there was a temporary change for a few hours in 1974, when props were brought in and the station used as a set for the film *Journey Into Fear*.
From the rear, a passage funnelled passengers to trains (or alternatively to Granville Street) via an over-track bridge (Fig. 45). A renovation in 1977 brought a new bridge which led instead to the Sea Bus terminal at the water's edge.

As part of the terminal for the Sea Bus to North Vancouver, plus the possibility that it could also become a ready-made rapid transit facility, the Canadian Pacific's station would appear to have a secure future. Boutiques and business offices are further revitalizing the building, and it is hard to realize that when the new Granville Square tower was built next door in the early 1970s, demolition was planned for the station. One is increasingly aware of the uncivilized folly of destroying heritage architecture still structurally sound.

Perhaps even more worthy of rescue from barbarity was the Great Northern Railway's Vancouver terminal, constructed in 1915. That splendid station (Fig. 46) replaced a ramshackle wooden depot on Pender at Columbia Street. The new site was on Main Street, using land reclaimed from tidal flat, earth-filled to a depth of over a dozen feet.

Architect for the Great Northern station was Vancouverite Frederick L. Townley (1887-1966) freshly graduated from the University of Pennsylvania.

Fig. 43   Vancouver, CPR III (1912-14) by Barrott, Blackader & Webster.

Fig. 44   General Waiting Room and Lobby of Vancouver CPR III.

Fig. 45   Track Side of Vancouver CPR III.

The GNR terminal was Townley's first large commission, and an important step to a long and successful career. The Vancouver City Hall (1936), the Stock Exchange, and several hospitals in the province of British Columbia are all to his credit.

The GNR Union Station (the Northern Pacific shared it for several years) was undisputably the most suave and elegant of the Vancouver terminals. A skin of granite, red brick and terracotta covered a skeleton of reinforced concrete, and within the palatial structure lay a spacious waiting room panelled in Alaska marble. Floors were also of marble, and molded lighting fixtures set off ornamental ceilings. Other touches of refinement included the provision of an exhibition room, and a glass-covered concourse leading to the umbrella-roofed platforms.

Finished in 1917, the terminal immediately had troops moving through it, and in the years following patronage by the general public was considerable. In the 1950s, railway passenger traffic slackened to the point where operation of the station was no longer economically feasible, so service was transferred to the Canadian National terminal next door. Demolition was carried out in 1964 to avoid further high tax assessments.

The hesitancy of railway companies to enter union terminal agreements was touched upon in an earlier chapter, and the obstinacy was no better demonstrated than in Vancouver, where two large stations rose almost concurrently not a hundred yards apart. It is, of course, understandable that independent stations left each company free to operate as it saw fit, and that the terminals stood as monuments to and advertisements for the might and worth of each company, but on economic grounds it seems difficult to justify.

Fig. 46   Great Northern's Union Station, Vancouver, B.C. (1915) by F. L. Townley.

Naturally enough, civic pride was boosted another notch with the building of each new terminal, and cheers greeted the first train arriving at the Canadian Northern station (Figs. 47-50) on the second of November, 1919. The 300 foot-wide head type terminal had cost over a million dollars to build, and its classic forms appeared truly majestic.

The Vancouver Canadian Northern terminal was R. B. Pratt's most ambitious station project. As at Winnipeg, a triumphal arch motif marked the main entrance, centred on the front facade. Unlike the Winnipeg design, however, was the marked verticality of the arch and the greater sobreness of the total effect. There were no Art Nouveau canopies or the like to soften the general appearances.

A schematic ground floor plan is shown in figure 47, outlining space allocation as it was in the building when first built. As with most stations, rearrangements have been considereable in the years following. The waiting room has been little changed, but almost everything else has been moved or adjusted.

Interior decoration in the CNR terminal matched the exterior in classicism and formality. Polished marble wainscotting and Caen stone lined the main walls, and fine ornamental plaster covered ceilings (Fig. 49). Carved, golden oak benches graced the general waiting room, and a long train shed completed the creature comforts. The original shed has been replaced by a few simple butterfly type platform covers (Fig. 50) but the grandeur of 1919 still lingers overall, and the city can continue to count the building amongst its architectural treasures.

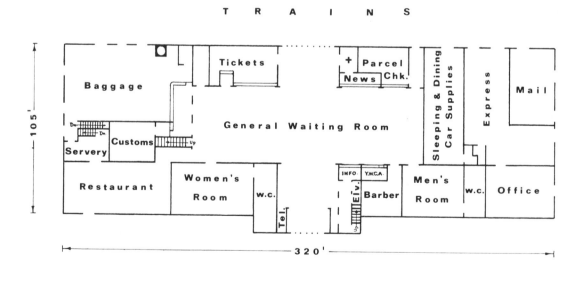

Fig. 47   Plan of Main Floor, CNR Vancouver (1919).

Fig. 48   Vancouver, B.C., CNR Terminal (1916-19) by R. B. Pratt.

Fig. 49   Ornamental Ceiling, General Waiting Room, CNR Vancouver.

Fig. 50   Modern Butterfly Type Platform Covers, CNR Vancouver.

THE CANADIAN NORTHERN FAMILY

Stations of the Canadian Northern Railway owed their family resemblance largely to R. B. Pratt, who prepared nearly all the plans. But the story of CNR stations actually began with a small group of depots in the Dauphin area of Manitoba, constructed shortly before Pratt became official architect for the railway in 1901. One of these stations was Laurier (Fig. 51) dating to 1899.

If the design's partially-hipped gable facing the tracks, twin upper trackside windows, general proportions and short canopy suggest the influence of standard stations of the Qu'Appelle, Long Lake & Saskatchewan, and the Calgary & Edmonton railways (see Fig. 25) it should not be too surprising. Contractors for the QALL&SR and the C&ER were the same canny Ontarians, Mackenzie and Mann, now heading their own railway, the Canadian Northern.[18] Exactly who the architect was for this pioneer CNR depot remains a mystery, for all existing early plans are unsigned. In keeping with western Canadian station tradition, accommodation was provided for an agent and his family. A kitchen and living room lay behind the station's business facilities, and three bedrooms were arranged upstairs. Only a partial basement was dug (mainly to contain a coal bin) but this was more than many small depots received. In total, the station set a tone of quiet robustness, sensible economy, and welcoming friendliness, that would be carried on in future depots of the company.

Fig. 51

In October, 1900 another important early plan appeared, which was for a combined station and section house (Fig. 52). Origins of the building's facade styling lay in the popular Gothic Revival cottages of the 19th century, which featured a steeply pitched and centrally placed dormer that abruptly interrupted the eaves line, and often contained a lancet window or a trefoil such as that seen here in this design. Ecclesiastical gothic elements like these were extremely rare in western Canadian stations, and did not reoccur in future on the Canadian Northern.

Floor plans (Fig. 53) show how the agent's domain was isolated from the section crew's. Railway rules forbade entry to station offices by any persons not on special business. That, of course, excluded section men ordinarily, for their duties lay outside, working on track and right-of-way. Strict order was necessary for safe handling of train movements, and in early days the agent sometimes handled large sums of money, so security was also a consideration. The absence of a waiting room in the plan was not too serious, for the building was intended for stops where few passengers could be expected, and a bench in the hall would normally suffice. For some points, however, business must have been greater than anticipated, because the structures were often modified to station-only use.

By 1901 the Canadian Northern was in a position to begin an expansion programme that would lead to transcontinental status in a relatively short time. Northern Pacific's Manitoba lines were acquired by the company that January, and the time was ripe for settlement of the northern prairies. For

TRACK SIDE ELEVATION

Fig. 52   Canadian Northern Combined Station-Section House (1900).

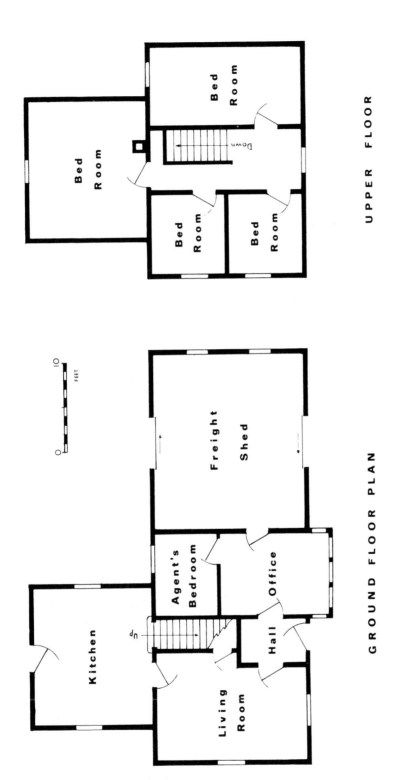

Bed Room

Bed Room

Bed Room

Bed Room

Down

UPPER FLOOR

Freight Shed

Agent's Bedroom

Kitchen

Living Room

Hall

Office

Up

10

0

FEET

GROUND FLOOR PLAN

Fig. 53   Floor Plans of CNR Combined Station-Section House (1900).

55

this grand scheme a number of large terminals, and a set of practical standard plans more distinctive and twentieth-century in appearance than those mentioned above, would be necessary. To Ralph B. Pratt fell the task of meeting these demanding requirements.

Pratt's first signed Canadian Northern station design appears to be that for special, end-towered depots to be built at St. Boniface, Manitoba, and Fort Frances, Ontario (Fig. 54). Essential elements of the standard designs that followed can be seen in this set of plans. Second-storey walls were shingled, lower ones sheathed with drop-siding. The trackside elevation (almost identical to that facing the street) featured a twin-windowed, central gabled dormer of 45 degree roof pitch, with a polygonal bay window below. The pyramidal roofed cube so obvious in the end elevation became the main

TRACK SIDE ELEVATION

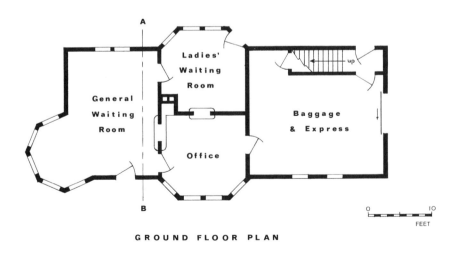

GROUND FLOOR PLAN

Fig. 54   Canadian Northern Station for St. Boniface and Ft. Frances (1901).

theme of the majority of small CNR depots. The unnecessarily complex star-form canopy brackets of the St. Boniface design saw no further use, probably for economy reasons, and the tower was also shunned in future by the Canadian Northern, though it achieved popularity on Canadian Pacific medium-size stations (Medicine Hat, Red Deer, Saskatoon, Vernon, etc.) either from its use previously on Maxwell's New Westminster (Fig. 17) or Pratt's Kenora station, both of 1899. The cross-section reveals typical structural and interior characteristics for stations of the period. Cedar posts formed a pile foundation, and no basement was included. Rooms had ten-foot ceilings both upstairs and down, and lower walls in the heavily used waiting room show wainscotting of vee-groove wood, although burlap was used in many standard stations.

END ELEVATION

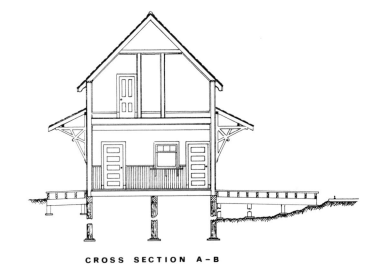

CROSS SECTION A-B

57

The Canadian Northern classified its stations into five main groups. Large, city terminals were designated First Class, and were inevitably special designs. The Edmonton station (Fig. 34) and the Vancouver terminal (Fig. 48) were in this category. Second, Third and Fourth Class stations could be either special or standard designs, but were usually the latter. The fifth group, combined station-section houses, were built only to standard plans, though sometimes modified in size and placement of freight room, as commonly occurred with the smaller stations.

Standard Second Class stations, which were of medium size and often contained a lunch room in addition to separate general and ladies waiting rooms, evolved from a few specials of the Vermilion type (Fig. 55). These were all of wood construction, except Neepawa, Manitoba (1902) which was for some unexplained reason built of brick. Lines, features, and general layout were all very much the same. Bay windows were placed on both track and street facades, the arrangement was symmetrical, and partial-hipped dormers sat on the wings. These last two features recalled the Laurier type, but a major improvement was the provision of a wide protective canopy on all four sides of the building. Metal finials on roof tips (later removed from almost all CNR stations) provided the only frills.

By 1910 a standard design, as exemplified by Stettler (Fig. 56) was ready. Here the dormers were given ordinary gables, and only one bay window, on the track side of the main floor, was included. Most of the remaining features were those found on the preceding models discussed above. Stuccoing was added to Stettler's exterior walls at a later date. A majority of the CNR's stations received this treatment in the 1920s and following as a means of economizing heat and maintenance costs. To protect lower walls from the blows of baggage wagons and the like, it was necessary to add horizontal wooden strips (called whaling) which happened to provide decoration as a bonus. Benches for all the stations were of lovely but unyielding oak (Fig. 63).

Standard Third Class stations were legion on CNR western lines, totalling well over 250 in all. The earliest plans (Fig. 57) dated to 1901. A perfectly pyramidal roof, and a lack of trackside waiting room windows characterized this version. The agent had convenient access to the freight room from his office, but the platform was more difficult to reach because it entailed crossing the entire waiting room diagonally, at times through waiting customers, to deliver orders to passing trains.

A revised, slightly longer Third Class type was introduced in 1907. The greater length disturbed the satisfying geometry of the roof somewhat. Waiting room space was increased, however, and a window on the track side did provide greater light and convenience for passengers awaiting trains.

Fig. 55   Canadian Northern's Vermilion, Alberta (1906). Street Side.

Fig. 56   CNR Stettler, Alberta (1911). Track Side.

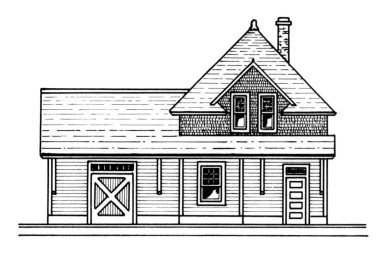

TRACK SIDE ELEVATION

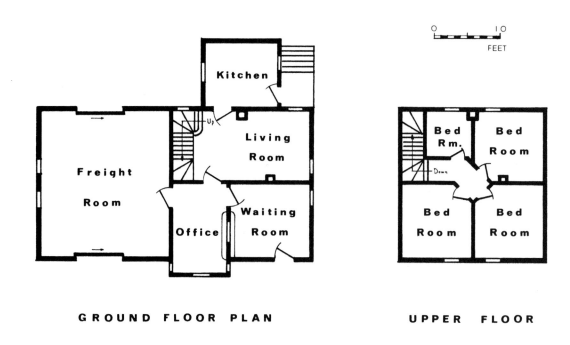

GROUND FLOOR PLAN

UPPER FLOOR

Fig. 57   Canadian Northern Standard 3rd Class Depot (1901 Version).

60

A further revision in 1915 reversed positions of waiting room door and window locations. An example of this final 3rd Class Canadian Northern standard is Smoky Lake (Fig. 58) except for stucco (added 1936) and washrooms (installed 1957, in the leanto at the right). The leanto on the left end of the building was intended as a coal shed, but the conversion to oil or gas heating in later years in many stations left the station agent with a little extra storage space for tools and other equipment. The general design of the station did prove satisfactory, for in 1929 it served as a basis for the Canadian National's standard of the same class.

Special stations based largely upon standard ones were built for places requiring perhaps greater waiting room space, a separate ladies waiting room, or a street entrance at the rear. One example was the modified Third Class depot for St. Paul, Alberta, which exteriorly resembled Smoky Lake in many respects, but in floor plan (Fig. 59) accomplished the above goals. Length could be added as shown here, or by additions to both sides of the main block, as occurred at Battleford, Sask. and a few other places. The same company style was maintained through proportioning, standard roof design and eaves brackets.

Fourth Class Canadian Northern standards were not numerous, and deserve little attention here for their architecture was of a rather low order. They consisted of a single-storey rectangular box with a gabled roof usually, which was in some cases extended at the front to form a canopy. The telegraph bay and canopy brackets (when used) resembled those of standard Third Class types.

The last main group of Canadian Northern standards was the combined station-section houses designed in 1912 and built near and through the sparsely-settled Rockies. The example at Galloway (Fig. 60) was typical for the first of two fairly similar versions. Ancestry lay in part in the 1900 design mentioned earlier (Figs. 52 and 53), part in the standard stations. A single gable facing the tracks interrupted the main roof's eaves line, but there was no gothic steepness to it. Styling of telegraph bay, brackets, doors and windows followed the 3rd Class standards. The floor plan (Fig. 61) separated agent's from section crew's quarters as usual, but a small waiting room on the station side improved upon the 1900 design. The upstairs contained two bedrooms for the use of section men.

One final note may be made regarding the special stations at Estevan, Hope and Chilliwack (Fig. 62). Although they resembled the above standards closely, they were by John Schofield. Schofield (1883-1974) became draftsman for the Canadian Northern in Winnipeg about 1907, after emigrating from his native Ireland. As architect for Canadian National in Montreal after the creation of the new company in 1920, he was ultimately involved with the design of the majority of CNR stations and hotels before his retirement in 1948.

Fig. 58   CNR 3rd Class Depot (revised type) at Smoky Lake, Alta. (1919).

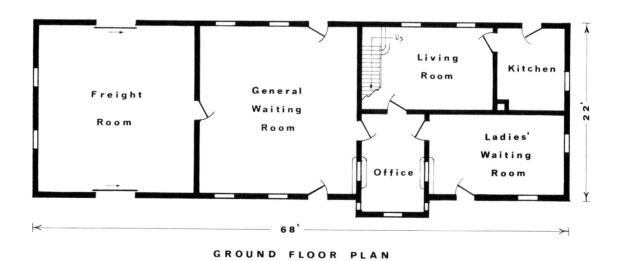

GROUND FLOOR PLAN

Fig. 59   Ground Floor Plan of CNR St. Paul, Alberta (1921).

Fig. 60   CNR 1912 Combined Station-Section House at Galloway, Alta.

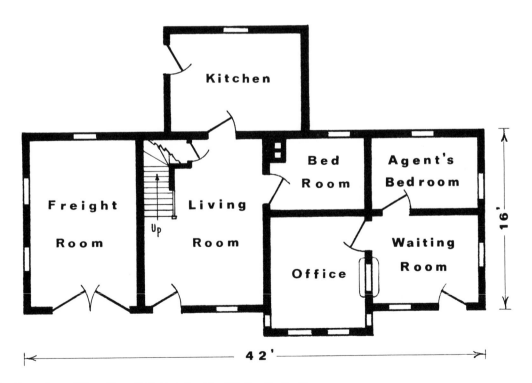

Fig. 61   Ground Floor Plan, CNR 1912 Combined Station-Section House.

Fig. 62   CNR Chilliwack, B.C. (1915) by John Schofield.

Fig. 63   Standard Canadian Northern Station Bench.

THE GRAND TRUNK PACIFIC FAMILY

Although the Grand Trunk Pacific spent lavishly on its trackage, and proclaimed itself "The Best Railroad Ever Constructed" in newspaper advertisements, GTPR stations were seldom superior to those of its competitors. The string of wooden depots that dotted the route from Winnipeg all the way to the coast used the same basic materials as the other major railways, and economy was unashamedly exacted at each and every opportunity. Prince Rupert was provided with the smallest and least exciting of any railway terminal on the Pacific, and while the Winnipeg station (Fig. 29) was impressive, it was built in collaboration with the Canadian Northern, on whose land it lay.

Medium-size depots with offices on their second floors were placed at divisional points. One of these was at Melville, Saskatchewan (Fig. 64) where branch lines were to run to Regina and Fort Churchill. Half-timbered gables and the use of eyebrow windows in the attic relieved the austerity of the design, which was again used at Rivers, Manitoba (c.1910) and Sioux Lookout, Ontario (1911). Less decorative stations of similar form and proportions were built at Edson, Alberta (1910), Reditt, Ontario (1912) and Smithers, British Columbia (1919).

For the subdivisional points of Biggar and Wainwright (situated between Saskatoon and Edmonton) large single-storey depots were constructed. GTPR Biggar still stands, but Wainwright (Fig. 65) was destroyed by fire in 1929 and had to be replaced. The 1909 design had a particularly handsome bell-cast roof recalling early Quebec houses. Also noticeable was the use of straight rather than curved canopy brackets, a habit of the company whenever brackets were used.

The design for Unity, Sask. (Fig. 66) was employed with various modifications at several points on the prairies, and along the National Transcontinental Railway in Ontario. The freight shed was usually integrated with the passenger station, but as we see here Unity had facilities that were separated. Note also that the freight shed has remained in its original, unstuccoed condition, unlike the station house. A unique feature of this station design was a flat portion of roof over the waiting room, hardly detectable when seen from the ground. The canopy brackets are also invisible from a distance. Support for the canopy is provided by rafters run onto extended joists (Fig. 67), an idea probably taken from mid-nineteenth century Grand Trunk stations in Ontario (Fig. 68). This element, combined with a remarkable clarity of articulation and slimness of proportions

Fig. 64   Grand Trunk Pacific Railway's Melville, Sask. (1909).

Fig. 65   GTPR's Wainwright, Alberta (1909, destroyed by fire 1929).

Fig. 66   Grand Trunk Pacific's Unity, Saskatchewan (1909-10).

Fig. 67   GTPR Eaves Supports (1910).

Fig. 68   Eaves Brackets, GTR Ernestown, Ontario (c.1854).

Fig. 69   GTPR Standard Station at Nokomis, Saskatchewan (1907).

produced a series of stations not confusable with those of any other company.

A small standard station (Fig. 69) designed in Montreal in 1907 for use on the Grand Trunk Pacific strongly resembled Canadian Pacific's standard number five (Fig. 39) which had appeared at least two years earlier on the CPR-controlled QA,LL&SR at Hanley, Sask. The Grand Trunk Pacific's management must not have been pleased with the likeness, for Nokomis appears to be the only example of this design on GTP lines.

The most popular GTPR standard station, known as Design A, was drawn in 1910 by some anonymous architect under K. B. Kelliker, chief engineer for the railway. This 16 by 52 foot depot (Fig. 70) was eight feet shallower than the Nokomis type, but was of about the same length. It was built at approximately 300 locations, and formed roughly two-thirds of the total GTPR station roster.

The Design A station could be used as a combined station and section house, with the freight shed serving as a bunk room for section crews. This accounts for the lack of any direct access to the freight room from the office in the standard plan (Fig. 71). When built for use as a regular station, a door was placed between living and freight rooms, although this meant that the agent continually traversed his living quarters during business hours if he wished to avoid going via the platform on wet or cold days.

Fig. 70   GTPR Standard Design A Station (1910) at Coleville, Sask.

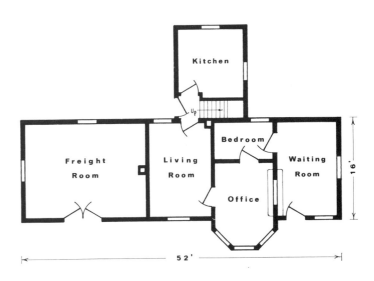

Fig. 71   GTPR Standard Design A Floor Plans (1910).

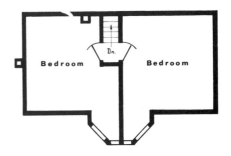

Heating in early years was by stove. A radiant type warmed the waiting room, a caboose heater served the living room, and a wood-burning cook stove thawed the kitchen. The two upstairs bedrooms were, like those in many prairie homes, unheated and definitely chilly in winter. In later times, oil and gas heaters replaced the original equipment, improving comfort considerably throughout.

Two standard GTPR stations appeared in the last few years of the company's existence, one in 1917 and the other in 1919. About ten depots were built to the 1917 plan, exemplified by Three Hills, Alta. (Fig. 72). Its most noticeable feature was an unusually high eaves line, which was made even more awkward by the interruptions of tall-windowed dormers. Straight eaves brackets supported the canopy formed by the extended flare of the roof. Styling generally matched that of most other preceding standards, but was much less well balanced.

The final standard plan, of 1919, was for a squarish, very plain two-storey house with a leanto telegraph bay on the front. It lacked either canopy or brackets, and resembled no other stations of the company. Fourteen of these supereconomical depots were constructed, at Wakaw, Gilroy, Avonhurst, and other points in Saskatchewan, Alberta, and British Columbia. The railway's romantic vision of a northern Eldorado had vanished in the turmoil of 1914-18, and with the nationalization of 1920 the Grand Trunk Pacific formally disappeared.

Fig. 72   **Grand Trunk Pacific's Three Hills, Alberta (1919).**

THE SMALLER RAILWAYS

Numerous small railways in the Canadian West simply hauled logs or minerals, and if they had stations at all they were of the most ordinary kind and not of any great size. Still other railways, generally of medium size, were built to develop and supply new and growing areas of settlement. Some of these companies and their stations merit discussion here.

The Esquimalt & Nanaimo Railway, Vancouver Island's largest, was begun in 1884. Regular passenger service between the two cities in the company's name was inaugurated in September 1886, and eventually rails reached Wellington (1887), Victoria (1888), Port Alberni and Cowichan Lake (1911) and Great Central (1925). Since the mid 1950s, when passenger service to Port Alberni ended, stations of the E&NR have been in decline. The Victoria station was demolished in 1972, and the Canadian Pacific (which acquired E&NR assets early in the century) applied in 1978 to end all passenger service as soon as possible. Thus the era of railway stations on the entire island appears to be coming to a close.

Stations of the E&NR differ markedly from those of the parent company, even though most of the depots date to after the takeover. The man mainly responsible for the company's designs was the chief engineer, R. A. Bainbridge,[19] whose offices were located in Victoria.

Largest of the surviving E&NR stations is the 1920 Nanaimo terminal (Fig. 73). Its quite original design included cedar wall shingling on the base contrasted with stucco above. The central block, well modulated and varied, was step-gabled and mansarded, then given extra color and continuities through the use of red brick edges and lintels. The station when built was undoubtedly the best on the island architecturally.

Parksville (Fig. 74) is a typical example of small E&NR depots, whose high freight rooms rise above the rest of the building. A prime reason for this feature was the need for elevated storage facilities in an unusually damp region. Cedar shingles, an abundant local material, were applied generously to walls and roofs, adding to the quiet charm and environmental harmony so characteristic of the majority of the company's stations.

On the mainland, one of the most promising railways of the early century was the British Columbia Electric. Of the four electric interurban railways in the Canadian West, the BC Electric was by far the largest, having 240 miles of track by 1914.[20] Besides street car service in Victoria, Vancouver and New Westminster, the BCER operated interurbans from Vancouver east to Chilliwack and south to Steveston. At the height of the interurban era

Fig. 73   Esquimalt & Nanaimo Railway's Nanaimo Station (1920).

Fig. 74   E&NR Station at Parksville, British Columbia (1911).

there were even plans to lay track all the way to Bellingham, in Washington State.

In Vancouver, the main terminal for the BCER was a five-storey structure at the corner of Carrall and Hastings streets (Fig. 75). General offices of the railway were located in the upper floors of the classicized 1911 edifice. It replaced an earlier, simpler, and smaller brick building at the same location.

At New Westminster, an angular brick terminal with iron cornice was likewise replaced in 1911 by a larger station in what might best be described as Renaissance Industrial style. Classical round arch windows and a wide cornice band ornamented what was otherwise a very ordinary two-storey brick building. As in Vancouver, and indeed many other North American

Fig. 75   Main BCER Terminal in Vancouver (1911) by Somervell & Putnam.

73

interurban stations, the cars passed through the buildings at street level — a convenience made possible by the use of clean, electric propulsion.

Most decorative of the small BCER stations was the Lulu Island line Vancouver terminal (Fig. 76) built at the Granville Street bridge in 1913. The Tudor-styled station, which had an octagonal cupola adorning its roof, held waiting and refreshment rooms plus offices for operating staff.

The rest of the BCER's small stations were relatively plain, and little different from depots of the steam railways. The Huntingdon depot (1909) differed little from CPR number five, and the single-storey standards for Langley, Prairie, Cloverdale, Maple Grove and Abbotsford featured clapboard bases with shingles above, a popular ensemble for minor stations everywhere in America in the early twentieth century.

Fig. 76   BCER Lulu Island Line Terminal in Vancouver (1913).

Far to the North, a narrow-gauge steam railway, the White Pass & Yukon, began regular service from Skagway on the coast to Whitehorse in the interior, on 15 August 1900. The thinly populated country through which the WP&YR passed needed relatively few stations, and none were made elaborate. The major terminal at Whitehorse could be reached by comfortable parlour cars (Fig. 77) but as can be seen, the station was devoid of decoration of any kind, a mere two-storey frame box without so much as canopy brackets. An improved station, of squared varnished logs later replaced this early austere building. Further architectural discussion of the company's stations, however, is not justified.

In 1912, another railway with sparsely-settled territory to serve was begun in northern Alberta, from Edmonton to Slave Lake. The Edmonton,

Fig. 77   White Pass & Yukon's Whitehorse Station (1900).

Dunvegan & British Columbia Railway (later part of the Northern Alberta Railway) built mainly wooden depots, but one in Edmonton, on the Saint Albert Trail, is said to have been of red brick.[21] The standard station for Berwyn (Fig. 78) gives a general idea of what the ED&BCR possessed. Inside, a small "hot room" for protection of certain merchandise against freezing was provided, for freight rooms and sheds were seldom heated in stations as a rule. In a region where minus forty degrees is commonplace in winter, the need for at least a small heated storage space was necessary, to say the least.

After the CPR gained a 50% interest in the NAR in 1928, the Canadian Pacific's standard 14A plans were sometimes used, Rycroft and Mclennan being two (modified) examples. The Canadian National, the other partner in the NAR, appears to have had little effect on NAR station design.

A third fairly large railway in the Northwest was the Pacific Great Eastern (now the British Columbia Railway) begun shortly after incorporation in 1912. The Canadian Northern's Vancouver station was to have been the southern terminus for the PGER, but for various economic reasons the idea never became a reality, and Squamish was chosen instead.[22] Despite slow progress in early years, the lines reached as far north as Dease Lake near the Yukon border by the 1970s, making the railway as important to the province as the CN or CPR.

Pacific Great Eastern stations were not exactly palaces, but their construction was of good quality, and design varied enough from other railways' depots to make the PGER distinctive. Clinton, shown in figure 79, represents one of the best early stations. Specifications on the plans called for all materials to be "first class in every respect . . . all workmanship . . . equal to the best", and these were closely adhered to. Drop siding covered the exterior, while indoors vee-groove lumber lined both walls and ceilings. Some rooms had varnished walls, doors and trim, giving a decidedly woodsy atmosphere. Others, including the waiting room, were painted. All floors were oiled, and lighting of office, waiting room and express section was by gasoline lamp. Needless to say, this was a perfect recipe for disaster by fire, but fortunately that did not occur here, although it was far from uncommon in wooden stations generally.

Track Side

Fig. 78   ED&BCR's Standard Depot at Berwyn, Alberta (1922).

Track Side

Fig. 79   Pacific Great Eastern's Clinton, B.C. Station (1915).

77

DEVELOPMENTS AFTER 1920

Only about a tenth of the stations in western Canada are of post-1919 date, for the great railway boom that had marked the beginning of the century was moribund before the war's end. Canada, its growth disrupted by the european hostilities, was forced into a calmer rate of expansion, slowed to a standstill in the depression of the 1930s.

Economies in construction in the post-war period are at once evident in the gradual abandonment of columns and polished marble slabs for large stations, and in the progressively plainer woodwork of the smaller depots. The art of station building did not die, however, for architects and engineers found new materials and methods of construction that could produce results both functionally clever and visually pleasing. The new crop of stations therefore did enlarge the list of architecturally interesting buildings in the Canadian West.

The Canadian Pacific's new Moose Jaw station (Fig. 80) situated at the head of Main Street where its attractive tower could be easily seen, was one of the last large terminals the company would build. The street entrance opened into a short concourse leading to the tracks. Ticket and baggage facilities were ranged along the walls to the right, while to the left a large portal led to the great hall (Fig. 81) containing waiting room and restaurant. A four-storey office building adjoining the passenger terminal housed baggage storage and telegraph departments on the ground floor, divisional offices above. A low wing was later added to the west end, along the tracks, to accommodate express services. The total result was a highly irregular floor plan, which was already trapezoidal because of the differing angles of street and track approaches (Fig. 3).

On the exterior, grey limestone was complemented by red brick. Deeply rusticated stone corners and lower walls, Roman arches, dentils, low roofs and Italianate tower created an effect very reminiscent of mid-nineteenth century railway architecture. The most startling feature, perhaps, was the brutal, heavily rivetted steel entrance canopy, that reminded the viewer that this was the age of machines, not humanism. Behind the station, track platforms were left without covers, indicating it seems the changed financial climate of the times more than the dryness of the region.

As can be seen in figure 81, the station's interior walls were boldly frank. There was no effort to disguise the yellow brick that rose in vast expanses above the cream-colored ceramic dado. A ceramic entablature and panels served to decorate the upper areas, and heather brown tiles on the floor completed the mellow scheme. The bronze war memorial plaque by

Fig. 80   CPR Moose Jaw, Saskatchewan (1920) by Hugh G. Jones.

Fig. 81   General Waiting Room, CPR Moose Jaw (1920).

Archibald Pearce, set midway along the waiting room's wall was a common feature in important CPR stations from the 1920s onward.

Architect for Moose Jaw CPR III was Hugh G. Jones (1872-1946). American born and trained, Jones became a CPR architectural designer in 1908, and remained connected with the railway after he established his own firm in Montreal in 1912. His design for Moose Jaw can be said to be clean in line, and structurally quite adequate, but it must be admitted that the visual appeal is not superior to the earlier building by Maxwell (Fig. 15).

Major western replacement stations on the Canadian National Railways in the 1920s were Jasper (1925) and Edmonton (1928).

The $30,000 Jasper station (Fig. 82) was a sequel to the construction in 1923 of the CNR's Jasper Park Lodge, a luxury holiday resort a few miles east of Jasper townsite. The station itself has an air of tidy informality. Its style followed in great part that of country houses built in England just before the war of 1914. Several of these had received acclaim in the Arts & Crafts circles, and illustrations appeared in such widely circulated periodicals as *The Studio* around 1912. The assymetrical, eaveless roofs of Jasper station are very much in keeping with those designs, as are the stucco, the uncut cobblestone lower walls, and the small-paned windows. On the interior, intentionally rough plaster between exposed beams of walls and ceilings contributed to a general domestic cosiness. A huge fireplace cheered hungry travellers in the restaurant, unfortunately now replaced by an ordinary coffee shop. Gone too is the bakery, and the large staff that was once housed in the station's upper floors.

Edmonton's new CNR station (Fig. 83) opened for traffic in March, 1928. Architect for the somewhat Doric edifice (there were single large columns of that Order to each side of the entrance) was John Schofield. Dark red brick covered most of the concrete shell, adding much-needed color.

The convenient, up-to-date restaurant featured a U-shaped lunch bar with revolving stools, speeding service to those anxiously awaiting trains, and a few regular tables were also available for more formal dining. This arrangement gained wide popularity in Canadian station lunchrooms in the 1920s and the idea has survived in many terminals.

Edmonton CNR II was designed as a hollow rectangle, whose central skylit concourse was bordered by a long restaurant on one side, and ticket and most other facilities on the other. Above these, on the second floor, were railway offices. It will be observed that Schofield was daring in his plan, for the long axis ran at right angles to the tracks. While this meant a greater distance to travel from street to trains, the architect believed that side motions would be minimized in such an arrangement, smoothing traffic flow.[23]

Fig. 82   Canadian National's Jasper, Alberta Station (1925).

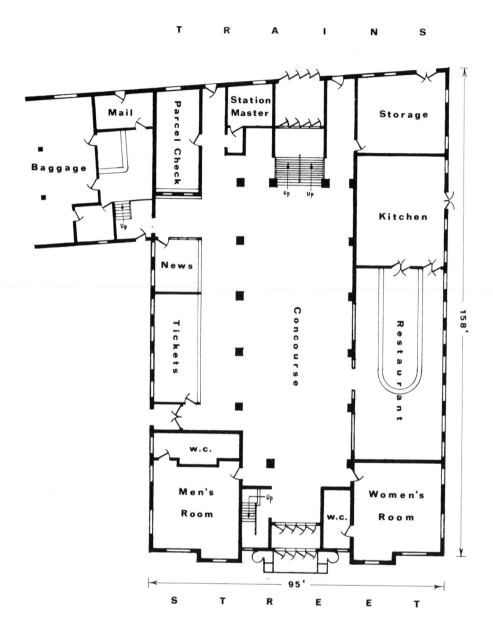

Fig. 83   CNR Edmonton, Alberta (1928). Ground Floor Plan.

Fig. 84   Union Station at Regina, Saskatchewan (1931).

Fig. 85   Waiting Room, Regina Union Station (1931).

The Regina Union Station (Fig. 84) was a product of the CPR offices in Winnipeg. Although first built in 1911, discussion has been reserved for this chapter because of the extensive reconstruction and enlargements of 1931-32, which brought it to the point in which it may be seen to-day.

The original 1911 Regina station was garbed in a rather free Italian Renaissance style, using heavily rusticated Bedford cut stone around the entrance arch, and deep reveals of windows and doors. Under the stone lay a reinforced concrete frame, a fire-resistant form of construction at that time finding favour in Canada.

The alterations of the early 1930s streamlined the styling, updating it to a classical Art Deco then fashionable. The CNR also adopted the style at this time, the 1939 Saskatoon station being one example. Dentils, pilasters and archways perpetuated the traditions of Greece and Rome, but the absence of capitals and the general flattening of surfaces proclaimed new twentieth century ideals of speed and simplicity. Interiors likewise followed the trend to lighter, less sculptured form, as can be seen in Figure 85.

In British Columbia, all stations constructed after 1920 were of smallish size. Some were not unusual, such as the CPR red brick station erected at Revelstoke in 1921. Its styling merely continued ideas employed a decade or more earlier at stations such as Red Deer. In the Okanagan, however, the 1923 Canadian Pacific depot at West Summerland (Fig. 86) showed more uniqueness. Its Mediterranean allure, accomplished by broad, simple forms and stuccoed walls, was in keeping with the sun-drenched area in which the station was located.

Canadian National's construction of the period in British Columbia was highlighted by special stations at Kelowna and at Kamloops, both built in 1926. At Kelowna, cobblestone, brick and stucco walls were topped by a flaring roof containing eyebrow attic windows that harked back to GTPR Melville (Fig. 64). The Kelowna depot, of only one storey, was relatively small but contained a Canadian Pacific ticket office in addition to the CNR facilities.

The Kamloops station (Fig. 87) a two-storey structure of red brick on a grey, cut stone base (Canadian Pacific's favorite materials for medium-size stations, curiously enough) is most noteworthy for its successful blend of Canadian Northern and Grand Trunk Pacific features. The quiet, neo-classical styling, the arrangement of two projecting, pedimented elements on the long facade, and the grouping of upper-storey windows in threes, closely echoed the CNR Brandon terminal of 1911 (Fig. 32). Heavy dentils in the cornice and pediments recalled those of CNR Vancouver (Fig. 48). Design of the canopy, brackets, and possibly the hipped roof can be seen to stem from GTPR stations such as Melville (Fig. 64). The artful composition achieved a remarkable harmony, but it was not used elsewhere.

Fig. 86   CPR West Summerland, B.C. (1923).

Fig. 87

CNR Kamloops, B.C.

            (1926).

Fig. 88   CPR Lloydminster, Sask. (1927).

TRACK SIDE ELEVATION

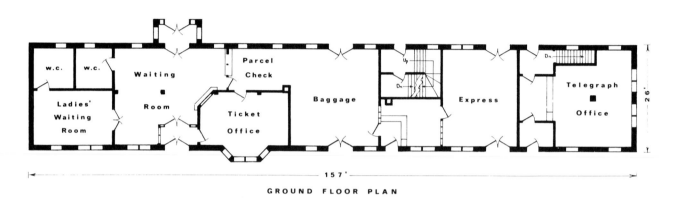

GROUND FLOOR PLAN

Fig. 89   Canadian National Railways' Le Pas, Manitoba (1928).

Fig. 90

GWWDR St. Boniface, Manitoba (1929).

Of Saskatchewan stations of the 1920-40 period, Canadian Pacific's Lloydminster (Fig. 88) was one of the most picturesque. The Tudorish depot sported an oriel and some half-timbering in its gables, which alleviated the plainness of the lower parts. Soon after the construction of Lloydminster depot, the design became standard A3.

In Manitoba, a special Canadian National station was built at Le Pas (Fig. 89) in 1928 to replace a standard Canadian Northern 3rd Class type that had served since rails first reached the town in 1910. Construction of the second depot coincided with the railway's extension on to the northern terminus at Churchill, on Hudson Bay.

The Pas CNR II, a hundred and fifty-seven feet in length, was half-timbered in the upper storey, while below lay brick on a newly standardized concrete base. Extra efforts were made to counteract the cold and damp of the region. Anterooms and entrance halls backed all but the freight entrances, in an attempt to minimize heat loss during the long, bitter winters. Special insulation for the structure included a layer of five-ply felt and pitch, an inch of waterproofing on inside walls, hair and felt between the studding, asphalt-coated insul board, and waterproof paper. Tenders for construction proved so high that the railway found it necessary to build the station itself.

At St. Boniface, an all-fieldstone terminal for the Greater Winnipeg Water District Railway took form in 1929 (Fig. 90). The style of the architecture, being a mixture of rough stone walls and traditional Georgian windows and entrances, much in the manner of many Empire Loyalist homes in southeastern Ontario, might be properly termed Frontier Georgian. Most activity on the GWWDR to-day entails gravel hauling, but mixed trains and occasional excursion specials continued to use the station in the 1970s.

In Alberta, two better than average stations were completed in 1930, one a brick structure for CPR Okotoks, the other a stuccoed edifice for CNR Vegreville.

The attractive depot for Vegreville (Fig. 91) was given dormers of Grand Trunk Pacific design (compare Fig. 66) but the concrete base and the stucco walls were features introduced by Canadian National. For special interest a *porte cochere* (a covered entrance) and an octagonal ladies waiting room were placed on the west end (Fig. 92). It should also be mentioned that a twin of the Vegreville station was built about two years earlier at Weyburn, Saskatchewan. Weyburn CNR was removed in the late 1960s, but Vegreville survived and now serves as a senior citizens' recreation centre, with only a small office reserved for railway use.

New sets of standard Third and Fourth Class station plans were prepared by the Canadian National Railways' Winnipeg engineering office about 1926. Wooden siding was used on some of the first examples, such as Waskatenau (1928) but revised plans dated April, 1929 specified both stuccoed walls and concrete bases for the new standards. Room arrangement varied little from that of predecessor Canadian Northern standards, but in the new Third Class type, such as Scott, Sask. (Fig. 93) a small "hot room" for perishable goods was incorporated, and an extra window added to the front of the telegraph bay. Fourth Class standards were little changed, but did achieve a new solidity with their new materials (Fig. 94).

The Canadian Pacific also continued to develop new standard stations, many based to a great extent upon earlier designs. The Western Lines 14A of 1930 for instance followed closely the Number 14 plan of 1914. Other designs could be related, such as the 16A design of 1928, used at Neilburg (Fig. 95). Frame construction, with half-timbering in the gables was much favoured by the CPR well into the 1940s. The photograph, showing Neilburg on blocks, ready for removal in 1974, illustrates the sad fate of many small stations in recent years.

Interiors of the later standards continued to be wainscotted with varnished vee-groove lumber or painted burlap, as in earlier stations, and plans reveal closet space to be ever at a premium in the living quarters (Fig. 96). One new factor was the introduction of a "hot room", which we have seen coming into use in the 1920s on other railways as well. It will be noticed in the plan here that the door width between freight and heated room was wider than an ordinary doorway, four feet to be exact with a full seven feet of height, to accommodate easier movement of goods.

Standard stations as much as specials reflected the hesitancy in Canada to completely abandon historicizing elements. As we have seen, medieval half-timbering, oriels, splayed eaves, etc. continued to ornament stations through the inter-war period. There would not, in fact, be any great change until the late 1940s, when ideals of internationalism became fashionable, and technology of the early century advanced to economical mass production.

Fig. 91   Canadian National Railways' Vegreville, Alberta (1930).

Fig. 92   Detail of West End, CNR Vegreville (1930).

89

Fig. 93   CNR Western Lines 3rd Class Station (1929) at Scott, Saskatchewan.

Fig. 94   CNR Western Lines 4th Class Station (1929) at Denholm, Saskatchewan.

Fig. 95   Canadian Pacific 16A Station (1928) at Neilburg, Sask.

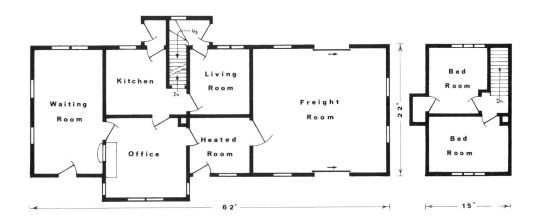

Fig. 96   CPR 16A Station, Ground and Upper Floor Plans.

91

Leaded Windows, CPR Lake Louise, General Waiting Room.

PART THREE

1940 - 1980

THE NEW ERA

Railways experienced heavy passenger volume during the Second World War but station construction remained limited because manpower and materials were directed to more important priorities. The end of hostilities did not, however, bring about any great surge in station building, quite the contrary. The railways had long been discontented with the high cost of maintaining passenger trains and terminals, a situation aggrevated by unstinting governmental support of highway and air travel. Skyrocketing labour costs and burdensome taxes constantly pressed the railways to cut trains and eliminate as many stations as possible. Station numbers therefore progressively fell as entire branches were either abandoned or converted to freight-only service. As could be expected, less begot less, and a public enchanted by ever flashier automobiles and speedier aeroplanes cared little about what happened to the rail systems.

The appearance of stations changed radically in the new era. In part, the rising costs governed the change, but also important was the wave of impatience with tradition that grew as technology advanced. Both form and materials in architecture were significantly altered in the profound upheavals in society and design. The Past fell into disrepute, the slow-moving civilizations of ancient Greece and Rome seemed more remote than ever, distressingly out of touch with the modern world's rapid movement, instant communication, mass production and powers of destruction. Great columns and arches, or quaint medieval architectural features seemed suddenly tiresome, supremely irrelevant, and Latin itself began to disappear from school curricula.

The change was not, of course, instantaneous. Deliberate picturesqueness lingered well into the '40s. One of the finest examples took form at Penticton (Fig. 97) in 1941. The Olde English flavour was far from negligible in the dark half-timbering set against sparkling white stucco. The small-paned windows, the steep roofs with their highly ornamental brackets and rafter ends (Fig. 98) all bespoke pre-war traditionalism in no uncertain terms. Nevertheless, and perhaps unfortunately, an end to such fantasy was close at hand.

International Style, which emphasized simplicity and stark geometry, eliminated historic allusion while promising more economical building. Whatever was not absolutely functional in the strictest sense was considered undesirable anywhere in or on the structure. Born of the union of Japanese domestic architectural precepts and European artistic revolt, nurtured by phenomenal industrial developments, and aided by an assortment of vocal architects on both sides of the Atlantic, the style made inroads everywhere

Fig. 97   Canadian Pacific Railway's Penticton, B.C. (1941-46).

Fig. 98   Under Eaves Detail, CPR Penticton.

during the 1920s and '30s. At Hamilton, Ontario, the 1932 station of the Toronto, Hamilton & Buffalo Railway, by New York architects Felheimer and Wagner, constituted the first use of the smooth, boxy style in Canadian railway architecture. The TH&B terminal remained, however, an isolated example for almost another decade, and only the occasional house, or public building such as Revelstoke, B.C.'s City Hall (1939) interrupted the general pattern of traditionalism before the war.

The International Style appears to have made its debut in western Canadian station architecture in 1941 (the same year the CPR was building the above Penticton station) with the designing of the Pacific Great Eastern's Shalalth depot (Fig. 99). The cubistic, flat-roofed, corner windowed structure emphatically dispensed with traditions as it ushered in the Age of the Box. It is questionable whether a land of jagged scenery and heavy precipitation is the appropriate place for horizontal roofs, but such considerations were brushed aside in the race to imitate what was being done in other parts of the world. The PGER's subsequent stations at Dawson Creek and Fort St. John (both 1950) with their gently pitched roofs, would seem to indicate a certain reassessment of appropriateness to environment, but the idea has doggedly survived up to the present in buildings of all types.

Fig. 99   PGER Shalalth, B.C. (1941). Track Elevation.

CANADIAN PACIFIC
STREAMLINES

Streamlining (smoothed and simplified shaping designed to reduce wind resistance, and ultimately derived from the great 20th century development, the aeroplane) was first employed by the CPR for its locomotives, beginning with the 4-4-4 Jubilee Class in 1936. In architecture, after blending modern with traditional forms in the 1930s (e.g. Regina, Fig. 84) the company decided to go a step further and try the International Style on the reconstruction of the Cranbrook, B.C. depot in 1945, as well as some other small, new depots in the East (Pendleton, Ontario for example, which opened in January 1946). In addition to the pure geometry given the Cranbrook station's forms, a color scheme of cream yellow with pea green trim was selected to replace the tuscan red with chocolate brown trim long used by the railway. Silhouette letters ousted the usual painted name board, and a slab canopy completed the new look.

The CPR's station at Field (Fig. 100) built in 1951, represented a slightly more elaborate structure in the new style. The slim, invisibly supported slab canopy, general handling of fenestration, and the use of fieldstone (could this have been an unconscious pun?) were reminiscent of the Burlington, Iowa depot of the Chicago, Burlington & Quincy Railroad (1944) by Holabird & Root.

On the end wall of Field station is a rare piece of railway equipment: a station bell, in use because of the sometimes lengthy stopovers for lunch, or clearances of snow or other debris in the mountain passes nearby. A few minutes before train departure, the bell is rung to warn passengers to reboard their coaches. Widely used in the early days of railroading to announce arrivals and departures, and still seen fairly commonly in Europe, the station bell is seldom found in North America to-day, for the locomotive's bell ordinarily serves the purpose now.

Calgary was the only large western city to receive new CPR passenger train facilities in recent years. The official opening of the station, which took place on the first of May, 1969, was somewhat unique as openings go, for it was highlighted by a junior vice-president of the company rolling out of sight aboard a cardboard carton on the luggage conveyor. The total office, shopping and transportation complex (Fig. 101) covers about two city blocks, but the station itself is quite tiny, occupying only a small, curved space around the base of the huge tower that supports the revolving restaurant. It illustrates well how the railway station has shrunk in importance in the West as a whole since the 1940s.

Fig. 100   Field, B.C. (1951). Canadian Pacific Railway.

Fig. 101   CPR's Palliser Square (at centre) Calgary, built 1966-69.

CANADIAN NATIONAL MODERNIZES

Modern styling was introduced to CNR station design by John Schofield's Central Terminal, built in Montreal in 1943, but innovation in the West was more or less restricted to materials for many years. The Churchill terminal's retention of several picturesque features (roof form, half-timbering, etc.) but use of asbestos siding demonstrates the general practice of the 1940s and 50s (Fig. 102).

The Prince Albert, Saskatchewan station of 1958 appears to be the first large box-style terminal in the Canadian West. It was a two-storey rectangle of concrete blocks, bricked on the exterior and glaze tiled on the interior. Aluminum was found useful for louvers, station name letters and canopy fascias. Both weather resistance (it never rusts) and machine age allure were factors in the choice of the light, polished metal whose use everywhere in the decade following the opening of large smelters at Kitimat in 1954 was indeed phenomenal.

The same materials were again selected for CNR Saskatoon in 1964, although aluminum was less in evidence (Fig. 103). Plexiglas, the darling of the '60s, ousted the metal as sign material. Facing of the concrete block with blue and yellow brick gave further color and refinement. Main support for the heavy, precast concrete roof members was the "old reliable", structural steel.

Colorful, slick surfaces were featured on the interior of this building (Fig. 104). Glazed brick, metal and glass walls, and fibreglass seats on stainless steel frames combined to produce an entirely new and decidedly cheerful effect in railway stations of the 1960s. Large window areas balanced the plentiful artificial surfaces with abundant natural light.

Color became the major instrument for the revitalization of older stations. The Canadian National's standard color scheme in 1949 consisted of a simple rust red on exterior walls, with cream doors, windows and trim. Roofs were black. Interiors tended to be rather earthy: creamy-brown walls, light cream sash and ceilings, sandy-brown dado, seats, doors and trim. Reliable, exact information on pre-war building coloration is unavailable but can be surmised from old photographs to have been quite plain. In the 1950s, livelier schemes appeared for many western CNR stations. The Borden, Saskatchewan depot, for example, received golden yellow exterior trim and a green door (roof black, stucco unpainted). Others, such as Scott (Fig. 93) had green eaves, brackets and outer window sash, the remaining trim being medium yellow. This scheme followed the livery used on new deisel loco-motives then coming into use. A change to even brighter colors came in the mid-1960s. Deisels were painted red, white and black. Stations such as Denholm (Fig. 94) were given brilliant orange-red doors (intense pale blue on freight doors) white eaves, black and white trim. Interiors were somewhat less gay: medium-grey walls and benches, white ceilings, white and black trim, but on the whole the impression was stimulating and the novelty welcome.

Fig. 102   Canadian National Railways' Churchill, Manitoba (1943).

Fig. 103   CNR Saskatoon, Saskatchewan (1964).

Fig. 104   Waiting Room, CNR Saskatoon.

Fig. 105   CN Tower, Edmonton (1966)

by Abugov & Sunderland.

The Edmonton terminal of 1966, located in the CN Tower (Fig. 105) was the last large CNR passenger facility built in the West. On the site of its predecessor, at the end of 100 Street, the elegant twenty-six storey building was well placed to direct bright red CN logos to the public below. A slight bow to the side walls may be observed, which the building's designers, Abugov & Sunderland[24] arranged to both escape the tyranny of the box (which had become rather oppressive by the mid '60s) and to gain extra space and light, i.e. it was the bow window on a grand scale. Also admirable was the smart contrasting of slim, white vertical cast stone members, with dark glass interspacings. Much of the tower is occupied by railway offices, though the company does not own the building. The train station is located in the basement, accessible by stairs, escalators, elevators, and a ramp. A bank and several other commercial enterprises occupy the remainder of the structure.

Interior arrangement of CNR Edmonton III (Fig. 106) forces passengers to split into two lines in order to pass the centrally placed elevators and ticket office. There is no distinct waiting room, benches are spread throughout the concourse. Any queues for tickets form in the quiet middle area. The open, informal plan is related to those used in contemporary air terminals, as is the baggage handling by conveyors and carousels.

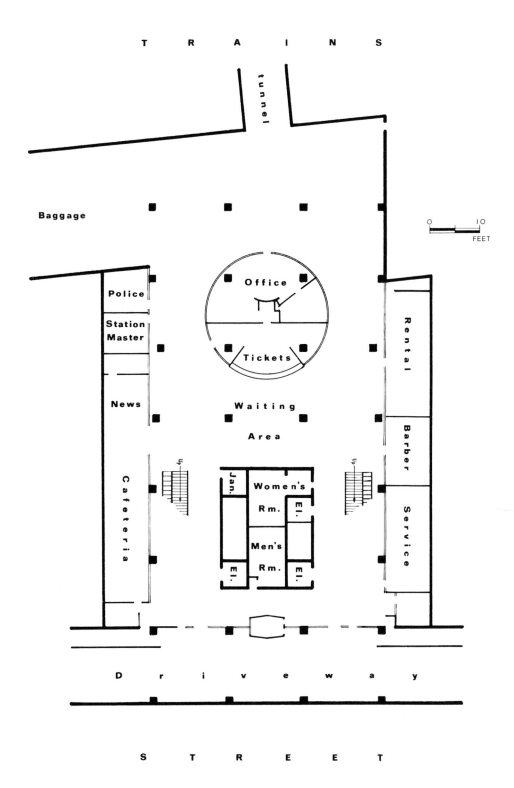

Fig. 106   Floor Plan of CNR Edmonton (1966).

Turning to small postwar western stations of the CNR, we find that unlike the Eastern Lines of the company, which built in the box style as early as 1945 (Midland, Ontario) the Western Lines preferred current vernacular house styling (Islay, Alta., etc.) right to the end of the 1960s. New siding materials, asbestos, aluminum, and vinyl were tried in turn on various depots, paralleling domestic usage, but roofs remained pitched, and design stayed homey.

The station at Houston, B.C. (Fig. 107) illustrates a change in trend, brought about in large part by the railway's increasing preoccupation with freight handling. The styling has much in common with warehouses and filling stations, and the smoothed rectangular masses trimmed with flat sheet metal are redeemed only by the use of vertically laid red cedar siding. Noticeably absent are the traditional railway station characteristics: a canopy and telegraph bay. Artificial lighting eliminated all fenestration from the freight room and the rear of the depot, which obviously dates to before the energy crisis. No further developments can be detected in the 1970s, and apart from the new, yellow brick station at Edson (1976) little happened in building activity in general on the system.

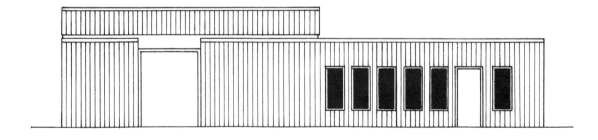

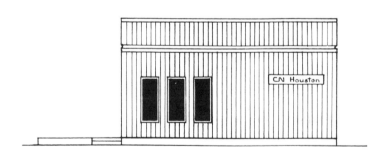

Fig. 107   CNR Houston, B.C. (1970). Track and End Elevations.

NEW P.G.E. and N.A.R. TERMINALS

From its earliest days, the Pacific Great Eastern Railway descended from the bush to the port of Squamish, from whence both freight and passengers were ferried by boat the remaining forty miles south to Vancouver. In August, 1956 the missing rail link along the rugged, rocky coast was finally made, and service carried directly into a gleaming new terminal at North Vancouver (Fig. 108).

The firm of Hale & Harrison[25] was engaged to prepare plans for this, the most important station on the railway. Clean lines, and easy track visibility for passengers were prime considerations, and since the relative warmth of the climate permitted practical use of completely glassed walls, a building closely following the precepts of the Bauhaus was a logical and appropriate choice. Reminiscences of the work of Mies van der Rohe (e.g. his German Pavilion at Barcelona, 1929) are clearly in evidence. The North Vancouver terminal is not large, less than 90 by 40 feet, yet one feels a remarkable freedom and ease thanks to the transparency of the front and side walls of the concourse. Offices have now replaced the coffee bar in the East end (Fig. 109) but other changes have been relatively slight. While this terminal has become well known to many inhabitants of British Columbia through the comfortable deisel railcar service to the north and central regions of the province, even greater fame has been acquired in recent years through the popular summer excursion trains that have left from here bound for Squamish behind former CPR steam locomotives.

The Northern Alberta Railway's Edmonton terminal of 1966 (Fig. 110) hardly compared in style or quality with the PGER's main terminal, and has remained virtually unnoticed on the northern outskirts of the Alberta capital. The economical, prosaic, prefabricated metal building was a far cry from anything resembling a chateau, and in reality constituted only a humble yard office, with a tiny counter by the door devoted to ticket sales to anyone willing to endure the slow, mixed freight trains that crawled northward to Waterways. Total discontinuance of passenger service, imminent by the mid 1970s would bring the railway full cycle in its passenger business, a situation perhaps not too far off for the whole industry. The lack of implied permanence in the building's appearance was typical of modern construction generally, and also characteristic was the emphasis on function over all other considerations. It seemed prophetic of the 1970s, in which not a single railway station would be built in Canada that had either remarkable beauty, size, or monumentality. Perhaps the circumstances and demands of the future will change this thoroughly deplorable state of affairs, let us hope so.

Fig. 108   PGER North Vancouver Terminal (1956) by Hale & Harrison.

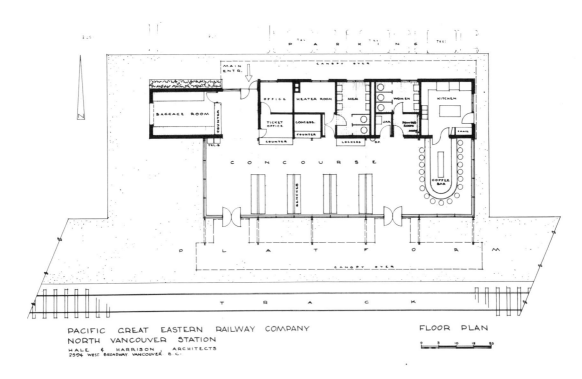

Fig. 109   Floor Plan, PGER North Vancouver Terminal.

Fig. 110   Edmonton Terminal (1966) of the Northern Alberta Railways.

Fig. 111   A Typical Small Railway Station Office in Western Canada.

ALL ABOARD!

After a century of constant technological advance, very little has remained unaltered in the operation of railway stations in western Canada. This in turn has had an effect upon the appearance and, sadly enough, the number of stations still to be seen.

To-day's station agent is, on the whole, far less busy than in former years, for passenger service has dwindled to near extinction, and milk handling, which once had enormous importance, is done mostly by truck. The only major concerns remaining are freight expedition and the transmission of Train Orders. Saturday and Sunday finds most stations closed, and weekdays they are kept open only during ordinary business hours. Some may be opened alternately half days by the same operator, and he (sometimes she) may even choose to commute from a nearby city rather than live in the station house.

With the refinement of electronic equipment, the telegraph key, once synonymous with railroading, has become obsolete and is now rarely used. To-day, information travels by telephone or radio from the dispatcher in each divisional office to operators in the respective stations, and in some instances messages may go directly to the trains themselves.

Despite the threat that full radio communication began to pose to the traditional system of train traffic control, there remained in the 1970s one aspect of operation which retained that certain romance surrounding station life: the hooping of written orders to engineer and conductor on moving trains. Very few orders by this date required a train to stop for signatures showing that the message had been received, so the station operator could thus generally be seen on the platform as trains arrived, holding out a hoop (or more likely a modern, high-speed fork) with a train order tied to the string between its prongs.

Since the 1880s, order boards have been mounted on most stations, usually above the telegraph bay, to notify train crews what kind of orders, if any, awaited them. Generally, these signals have been of the semaphore arm variety, but oval discs with lanterns on top were installed for a time by both the CPR (see Gleichen, Figure 5) and the GTPR (e.g. Coleville, Figure 70). Absence of an order board may indicate an obligatory stop, such as main terminals, junctions, etc., but old photographs sometimes reveal an absence of signals because the standard code for operating by train order was not adopted until 1887. It should be pointed out to those unfamiliar with railway practice, that order boards in no way indicate passengers wishing to board approaching trains. If that is desired, trains must be hailed by a side to side arm movement using green and white flags, or a lantern if at night. At some points a flag device resembling a saw horse is set at right angles to the track. Complete radio signalling will spell an end to all of this colorful hand-operated equipment, changing forever the look and character of the regular small depot.

Service reductions and line abandonments continued to threaten the very survival of railway stations in all of North America as the 1980s approached, and it will be unfortunate if the trend to station demolition or conversion to other uses continues. The former is the worst, beyond any doubt, for it represents an outright and permanent destruction of cultural heritage. The latter accomplishes preservation of a sort, but no matter how many baggage wagons, telegraph keys, or other paraphernalia are placed on display, the inimitable blend of ticking, clicking, ringing and chatter of an operating depot is lamentably lacking.

Do railway stations in western Canada indeed have a future? That question can not for the moment be answered with absolute certainty, but indications are not encouraging. The number of small stations is falling rapidly as centralization of freight handling and train control continues to increase. Shelters have already replaced some regular depots (Fig. 112) and bare ground is all that one finds at many other points. This reduction in service and choice of stops does not encourage the use of passenger trains, nor does the relocation of city terminals from downtown sites to ones on the outskirts (at Brandon, Saskatoon, etc.) make rail transportation more appealing. The lack of direct transport to the hub of urban transit, hotels, offices and stores makes both communting and long distance travel inconvenient, if not impossible. With these developments in mind, one can not view future passenger travel by rail with any optimism.

The establishment in 1978 of Via Rail, a crown corporation to operate passenger service over the CPR and CNR marked the beginning of a new phase in Canadian railway station history.[26] How long and successful it will be remains to be seen. It is not certain whether the railways will retain ownership of the stations, or whether the Government of Canada will ultimately take them over. Via Rail in any case began by leasing them from the railways, and employing the staff required to provide information, reservations, tickets and baggage handling. If the system is to operate with any degree of success, i.e. show a profit and be attractive to the public, it is rather obvious that it will be necessary for rail terminals, like roads and airports, to be directly financed and maintained by the government.[27] This would greatly reduce the competitive advantage already given road and air travel for too many decades, and release more railway revenue for much-needed service and equipment improvement.

In a land of long, hard winters when non-rail transport is often unreliable, and in the face of many serious problems associated with the over abundance of non-rail vehicles (road and airport congestion, danger and expense, high energy consumption, rising rates of respiratory diseases, dwindling agricultural space and non-renewable resources) it is imperative that the whole transportation question be given a serious examination. Passenger trains, given proper support can provide an ideal, comfortable, fast, reliable and efficient means of travel. It remains for the general public and responsible politicians to be brought to such a realization, and it is basically in their hands, and not the railways or the architects, that the future quality and quantity of railway stations in western Canada now rests.

Fig. 112   CNR Shelter at Innisfree, Alberta, replacing a Standard Canadian Northern 3rd Class Depot of 1906.

NOTES

1. Ponoka, Alberta's United Church was one of many instances (cf. *CPR Staff Bulletin,* February 1945, p. 16).
2. See T.D. Regehr, *The Canadian Northern Railway, Pioneer Road of the Northern Prairies,* Toronto: Macmillan, 1976, pp. 173-4.
3. Buffalo bones can be treated to produce phosphoric acid, an agent often employed to clarify raw sugar in solution.
4. See R.B. Wilson, *Go Great Western,* Newton Abbot: David & Charles, 1970, p. 157.
5. "Port Moody Loses Historic Buildiing", *Vancouver Sun,* 29 September 1961, p. 58.
6. The Chateau Frontenac opened 18 December 1893 (cf. H.D. Kalman, *The Railway Hotels & Development of the Chateau Style in Canada*), Victoria: University of Victoria Press, 1968, p. 11.
7. Edward Colonna (dates unavailable) was German-born, educated in Brussels, became a U.S. citizen in the 1880s and worked in Dayton, Ohio as a railway car designer before going to Montreal to work for the CPR. He later went to Paris to join Bing, the famous Art Nouveau furniture maker.
8. Edward Maxwell (1867-1923) began practice in his native Montreal in 1892, after a short association with the Boston firm of Shepley, Rutan & Coolidge. He was in partnership with his brother William (Note 14) from 1901 to 1922. The massive stations of the 1890s were all attributed to Edward alone in contemporary periodicals. Besides the western depots, were CPR Galt (1898) and Ottawa (1900) in Ontario, McAdam Junction, New Brunswick (1900) and part of Windsor Station, Montreal (1900).
9. The Hastings depot was by Thomas C. Sorby, of Sorby & Wilson, Victoria and Vancouver. Born in England, Sorby worked there in the 1860s as County Court Surveyor and consulting architect to the Home Office. In 1883 he moved to Montreal and began designing stations and hotels for the CPR. The CPR terminal buildings in Vancouver (1886) were his work, and the CPR depots in Figures 5 and 6 might conceivably be as well.
10. H.D. Kalman, *op. cit.,* p. 11.
11. Ralph Benjamin Pratt (1872-1950) of English origin, became a draftsman for the Canadian Pacific in Winnipeg in 1895, advanced to architect, then switched to the Canadian Northern Railway in 1901. His most important CPR station was probably the Rat Portage (Kenora) depot of 1899. The Vancouver terminal (1919) was his largest for the Canadian Northern. By 1906 Pratt had formed a firm of his own, but remained consulting architect to the CNR.
12. See *Canadian Pacific Staff Bulletin,* September 1947, p. 17.
13. See *Railway & Shipping World,* Nov. 1899, p. 324, Dec. 1899, p. 349.
14. William Sutherland Maxwell (1874-1952) brother of Edward (Note 8) studied at the Beaux Arts and Atelier Pascal in Paris 1899-1902. He gained experience with his brother 1890-93 and 1897-99, as well as with Winslow & Wetherell, of Boston (1893-96). The old Art Gallery of Montreal, Montreal General Hospital, portions of the Chateau Frontenac at Quebec, and the Saskatchewan Parliament Building in Regina were amongst his best known works.
15. The first Bush type shed (named after its inventor, Lincoln Bush, chief engineer for the Delaware, Lackawana & Western Railroad) was installed at Hoboken, New Jersey in 1905. See J.A. Droege, *Passenger Terminals and Trains,* pp. 35-42.
16. See "Calgary's Union Station", *Medicine Hat News,* 28 July 1910.
17. The other major art work at CPR Vancouver is the war monument by sculptor Coeur de Lion Mac-Carthy, unveiled in 1921. There are duplicates at CPR Winnipeg and Windsor Station, Montreal.
18. William Mackenzie and Donald Mann's extensive previous railway contracting had included the Midland division of the Grand Trunk Railway, parts of the Credit Valley Railway, the CPR short line through Maine to St. John, N.B., the Kicking Horse section of the CPR in the Rockies, several street railways and numerous other projects. Mackenzie was the first president of the Canadian Northern. See G. R. Stevens, *History of the CNR,* New York: Macmillan, 1973, pp. 171ff., and *Railway & Marine World,* Feb. 1909, p. 97.

19. R. A. Bainbridge (1864-1949) was born in England, went to work in Quebec at age 19, then moved to British Columbia, where he became CPR divisional engineer at West Kootenay, and later at Victoria. Bainbridge, B.C. may be named for him.

20. The Edmonton Interurban had eight miles of track, the Edmonton Radial fifty, and the Winnipeg, Selkirk & Lake Winnipeg Railway twenty-two (cf. *Canadian Railway & Marine World,* May 1915, p. 184). No documentation was available for stations of these companies.

21. A. W. Cashman, *The Edmonton Story,* Edmonton: Inst. of Applied Art, 1956, p. 33.

22. See T. D. Regehr, *Op.Cit.,* p. 327. The Pacific Great Eastern became the British Columbia Railway in 1972 (not to be confused with the B.C. Electric Railway, which is now known as the B.C. Hydro Railway).

23. "Edmonton Station", *Canadian Railway & Marine World,* April 1928, p. 188.

24. Architect Maurice Sunderland, a native of Northern Ireland, moved to Canada in 1954, and formed partnership with engineer Jack Abugov, a native of Ontario, in 1956. The firm specializes in large projects, such as Western Centre (Calgary) etc.

25. The PGER North Vancouver terminal was the first major commission for the firm. The partnership dissolved in 1961. Various commercial and municipal buildings around Richmond, B.C. are the work of Richard Hale, while Robert Harrison (principally responsible for the PGER Station) has had particular success with educational and apartment buildings (Parkwood Terrace, Burnaby having won a Massey medal).

26. See "Canada Goes Via Rail", *Railway Age,* 10 April 1978, pp. 32-34.

27. See Micheal Jackson, "Via - Off The Rails?", *Canadian Forum,* Vol. LVIII, No. 684, September 1978, pp. 6-9.

SELECTED BIBLIOGRAPHY

Barman, Christian, *An Introduction to Railway Architecture,* London: Art & Technics, 1950.

Berg, Walter G., *Buildings & Structures of American Railroads,* New York: Wiley, 1900.

Biddle, Gordon, *Victorian Stations,* Newton Abott: David & Charles, 1973.

Bohi, Charles, *Canadian National's Western Depots,* West Hill: Railfare, 1977.

Buel, Ronald A., *Dead End,* Baltimore: Penguin, 1973.

Carlisle, Norman, *The Modern Wonder Book of Trains and Railroading,* Philadelphia: Winston, 1946.

Droege, John A., *Passenger Terminals and Trains,* New York: McGraw-Hill, 1916, reprinted 1969 by Kalmbach, Milwaukee.

Ducey, Brant, *Canadian National Railway Stations in Edmonton,* Typescript: CNR Edmonton, 1964.

Educational Facilities Laboratories, *Reusing Railroad Stations,* New York, 1974.

Fleming, Sandford, *Report of Surveys & Preliminary Operations of the Canadian Pacific Railway to January, 1877,* Ottawa, 1877.

Hopper, A.B. and Kearney, T., *CNR Synoptical History,* Montreal: CNR, 1962.

Jenson, Oliver, *Railroads in America,* New York: American Heritage, 1975.

Kalman, Harold D., *The Railway Hotels & The Development of the Chateau Style in Canada,* Victoria: University of Victoria, 1968.

Meeks, Carroll L., *The Railroad Station,* New Haven: Yale U., 1956.

Regehr, T.D., *The Canadian Northern Railway, Pioneer Road of the Northern Prairies,* Toronto: Macmillan, 1976.

Stevens, G.R., *History of the Canadian National Railways,* Toronto: Macmillan, 1973.

Stone, T.R., *Beyond the Automobile,* Englewood Cliffs: Prentice Hall, 1971.

Wilson, Roger B., *Go Great Western,* Newton Abott: David & Charles, 1970.

INDEX

Note: Railway stations mentioned in this book are listed separately, following the general index.

Abugov & Sunderland, architects/engineers, 102, 113
Air terminals, 102, 110
Aluminum, 99, 104
Arches, 10, 17, 33, 34, 42, 50, 73, 78, 84, 94
Art Deco, 84
Art Nouveau, 34
Arts & Crafts, 80
Asbestos, 99, 104
Attics, 14, 42, 84

Baggage handling, 19, 33, 34, 78, 97, 102, 110
Bainbridge, R.A., architect-engineer, 71, 113
Balconies, 19
Balustrades, 36
Bandstands, 10, 17
Barrott, Blackader & Webster, architects, 46, 47
Basements, 34, 53, 57, 102
Bases, 14, 17, 38, 42, 71, 74, 84, 87
Bauhaus, 105
Bay windows, 9, 19, 22, 56, 58, 84
Beaux Arts (Parisian), 33
Beiseker, Alberta, 3, 5
Bellingham, Washington, 73
Bells, 97
Bell-cast roof, 65
Benches, 7, 33, 50, 58, 64, 99, 100, 102
Bessborough Hotel, Saskatoon, 4
Box style, 96, 97, 99, 102, 104
Brackets, 57, 65, 67, 70, 84, 94, 95
Branch railways, 26, 30
Brick, employment of, 10, 14, 17, 19, 33, 38, 46, 49, 58, 71, 73, 78, 80, 84, 87, 99, 104
British Columbia Electric Railway, 71
British Columbia Railway, 76, 113
Buffalo bison, 10, 112
Burlap, 57, 88
Bush type train shed, 34, 112

Calgary & Edmonton Railway, 26
Canadian National Railways, 30, 80
Canadian Northern Railway, 14, 30, 34, 53
Canadian Pacific Railway, 7, 26, 30, 71
Canopies, 7, 10, 17, 34, 58, 61, 70, 78, 84, 97, 99, 104
Cedar shingles, 71
Cedar siding, 104
Ceilings, 33, 49, 50, 52, 57, 76, 80, 99, 100
Centralization, 110
Ceramic, 78
Chateau Frontenac Hotel, Quebec, 14, 112
Chateau style, 14, 17, 33, 38, 105
Chicago Columbian Exposition, 33
Church usage of stations, 3, 112
Classical style, 10, 33-37, 42, 44, 50, 73, 84
Classification of C.Nor.Rwy. stations, 58
Clocks, 33, 36
Closets, 88
Cobblestone, 38, 42, 80, 84
Colonna, E., architect, 17, 112
Color, 71, 97, 99, 100
Columns, 33, 78, 80, 94
Combination stations, 7
Competition, 38, 45

Concourses, 49, 78, 80, 102, 105
Concrete, 34, 80, 84, 87, 88, 99, 102
Connaught tunnel, 13
Consoles, 36, 42
Copper, 17
Cornices, 44, 73, 84
Crookston, Minnesota, 10
Crow's Nest Branch, 26, 28
Cupola, 74

Dease Lake, B.C., 76
Demolition, 44, 46, 49, 88, 110
Design A (GTPR), 68
Dining Rooms, 10, 19, 34, 58, 78, 80, 105
Divisional points, 65
Domes, 34
Donald, British Columbia, 4
Doors, 7, 22, 58, 61, 68, 88, 99, 100
Doric Order, 80
Dormers, 17, 22, 28, 31, 38, 42, 54, 56, 58, 70, 87
Drop siding, 22, 23, 56, 76

Eaves, 61, 67, 70, 80, 88, 95, 100
Edmonton, Dunvegan & British Columbia Railway, 75
Edmonton Interurban Railway, 113
Edmonton Radial Railway, 113
Edmonton, Yukon & Pacific Railway, 38
Electric Railways, 71-74, 113
Elevators, 102
Empire Loyalist, 87
Energy, 104, 111
Engineering offices, 22, 71, 84, 87
English Domestic Revival, 45
Entrances, 7, 17, 34, 35, 42, 50, 61, 78, 84, 87, 89
Environmental harmony, 71, 96
Escalators, 102
Esquimalt & Nanaimo Railway, 71
Express handling, 7, 19, 38, 42, 71, 78, 104, 110

Felheimer & Wagner, architects, 96
Fibreglass, 99
Fieldstone, 87, 97
Film set, 46
Finials, 9, 58
Fire, destruction by, 19, 65, 76
Fireplaces, 22, 80
Flat roofs, 96
Fleming, Sandford, 3, 5, 30
Floor plans, 9, 24, 36, 50, 55, 56, 60, 63, 69, 82, 91, 103, 106
Floors, 34, 76, 78
Fort Churchill, Manitoba, 65
Frame construction, 10, 56, 65, 88
Freight rooms — *see Express handling*
Friezes, 34, 36, 46
Frontier Georgian, 87
Foundations, 7, 57
Furniture, 7, 10, 25, 33, 34

Gable treatment, 9, 19, 22, 38, 45, 61, 65, 71, 88
Gambrel roof, 13, 22
Gardens, 10, 17
Georgian features, 87
Glacier House, B.C., 12, 13
Glass, 92, 99, 102, 105
Gothic style, 28, 54, 61
Grand Trunk Pacific Railway, 30, 34, 65
Grand Trunk Railway, 30, 65
Granville Square, 46

Great Northern Railway, 46
Greater Winnipeg Water District Railway, 87

Hale & Harrison, architects, 105, 106, 113
Half-timbering, 42, 45, 65, 84, 87, 88, 94, 99
Hardwick, Philip, architect, 34
Heating, 61, 70, 76, 87
High Level Bridge, Edmonton, 44
Historicizing, 88
Holabird & Root, architects, 97
Hot Room, 76, 87, 88
Hotels, railway, 4, 13, 14, 19, 33, 36, 37
Hudson Bay, 87

Ictinus, 36
Indians, 10
Insulation, 22, 58, 87
Insul-brick, 22, 26
Intercolonial Railway, 30
Interiors, 33, 34, 49, 50, 57, 76, 78, 80, 84, 88, 99, 100
International style, 94, 96, 97
Interurban railways, 71

Jerkin-head roof — see partial-hip
Jones, Hugh G., architect, 79, 80
Joy, C.E., architect, 14

Kelliker, K.B., engineer, 68
Keystones, 36
King George VI of England, 42
Kitimat, British Columbia, 99
Kootenay Landing, British Columbia, 26

Land sales, 10
Langford, Adelaide, 46
Laurier, Wilfred, government, 30
Leaded windows, 19, 92
Lighting, 34, 76, 99, 102, 104
Link, Theodore, architect, 14
Living quarters, 7, 31, 53, 61, 88
Lobbies, 34, 46
Locomotives, 97, 99, 100
Log stations, 10, 11, 13, 75
Lulu Island Line, BCER, 74

MacCarthy, C. de L., sculptor, 112
Mackenzie & Mann, contractors etc., 26, 53, 112
Macleod, Alberta, 26
Manitoba Hotel, Winnipeg, 14, 15
Manitoba & North Western Railway, 14, 30
Mansard roofs, 13, 71
Marble, 34, 49, 50, 78
Maxwell, Edward, architect, 17, 18, 21, 33, 112
Maxwell, W.S., architect, 32, 33, 112
Minnedosa, Manitoba, 14
Montreal, Quebec, 19, 33, 46, 99
Monumentality, 19, 105

Name boards, 10, 13, 97, 99
National Transcontinental Railway, 30, 44, 65
Neo-Roman classicism, 33, 84
Northern Alberta Railways, 76, 105
Northern Pacific Railway, 14, 49

Office, Agent's, 4, 7, 22, 54, 61, 87, 108
Offices, divisional, 65, 78, 109
Offices, general, 19, 34, 73, 74, 78, 80, 102, 105
Offices, ticket, 17, 78, 80, 84, 102, 105, 110
Okanagan valley, 19, 26, 84

Order boards, 109
Oriel, 87

Pacific Great Eastern Railway, 76, 96, 105, 113
Palladian windows, vi, 38
Palliser Hotel, Calgary, 17
Palliser Square, Calgary, 98
Partial-hip roofs, 10, 25, 26, 53, 58
Pearce, Archibald, sculptor, 80
Pediments, 36, 84
Pembina Branch Railway, 10
Picturesqueness, 9, 22, 26, 87, 94, 99
Pilasters, 36, 42, 84
Pitched roofs, 104
Plaster, 52
Platforms, station, 22, 34, 38, 49, 50, 52, 78
Plexiglass, 99
Porches, 36
Porte cochere, 87, 89
Pratt, R.B., architect, 22, 24, 53, 56, 57, 112
Prefabricated stations, 7, 105
Price, Bruce, architect, 19
Prince Edward Hotel, Brandon, 36, 37
Pyramidal roofs, 56, 58

Qu' Appelle, Long Lake & Saskatchewan Railway, 26, 44, 53, 68
Quebec City, 30

Rafters, 65, 67, 94, 95
Rail travel, 110, 111
Railway Street, 3
Recreation centre, 87
Red River, 10
Relocation, 36, 110
Renaissance style, 73, 84
Restaurants, station, see Dining Rooms
Restaurant use, 6, 19
Revelstoke City Hall, 96
Rogers, A.B., engineer, 13
Rogers' Pass, 12, 13
Rohe, Mies van der, architect, 105
Romano, Giulio, architect, 36
Royal Alexandra Hotel, Winnipeg, 33

Sandstone, 17, 19, 42
Saskatchewan Legislature, 33
Schofield, John, architect, 61, 64, 80, 99
Scrollsaw work, 22, 23
Sculpture, 78-80, 112
Sea Bus, 46
Selkirk mountains, 12, 13
Sheathing, 22, 25, 57, 76, 88, 104
Shelters, 25, 110, 111
Shingles, 14, 19, 22, 56, 71, 74
Shuswap & Okanagan Railway, 26
Situation of stations, 3-6, 22, 46, 78, 102
Skylights, 34, 80
Slate roofs, 17
Somervell & Putnam, architects, 73
Sorby, T.C., architect, 112
Space allocation, 54, 58, 61, 68, 78, 80, 88, 102
Spanish Mission style, 28
Squamish, British Columbia, 76, 105
Stairs, 34
Standard stations, CNR: 61, 87, 88, 90. Canadian Northern: 56-63. CPR: 7, 8, 41, 42, 68, 76, 87, 88, 91. GTPR: 68-70, 108. NAR: 76, 77

Station conversion, 6, 19, 36, 42, 46, 87, 110
Station decline, 94, 105, 110
Station financing, 4, 10, 49, 80, 110
Station-Hotels, 14, 19
Station-Section Houses, 54, 55, 61, 62, 68
Station-Yard Offices, 105
Station naming, 4, 6, 10
Station operation, 22, 109-110
Station ownership, 102, 110
Steel, 34, 46, 78, 99
Steveston, British Columbia, 71
Stone, usage of, 14, 17, 19, 22, 33, 36, 38, 42, 44, 46, 49, 50, 78, 84, 87
Streamlining, 84, 97
Stucco, 38, 44, 58, 61, 71, 80, 84, 87, 88, 94

Telegraph bays, 9, 19, 22, 56, 61, 70, 88, 104
Telegraph key, 7, 109
Terracotta, 49
Tile, 78, 99
Towers, 17, 19, 26, 33, 38, 57, 78, 97, 102
Townley, F.L., architect, 46
Train orders, 109
Train sheds, 34, 50
Tudor style, 45, 74, 87
Turrets, 19, 38, 42

Union stations, 3, 34, 44, 45, 49, 84

Via Rail, 110
Vinyl, 104

Wainscotting, 34, 50, 57, 78, 88, 99
Waiting rooms, general, 7, 46, 47, 50, 52, 54, 57, 61, 78, 83, 92, 101, 102
Waiting rooms, ladies', 7, 19, 61, 87
War Memorials, 78, 112
Warren & Wetmore, architects, 34, 35
Washrooms, 34, 61
Water towers, 26
Waterways, Alberta, 105
Wellington, B.C., 71
Wetaskiwin, Alberta, 30
Whaling, 58
White Pass & Yukon Railway, 75
Windows, 23, 58, 65, 80, 84, 87, 92, 96, 99, 104, 105
Winnipeg, Selkirk & Lake Winnipeg Rwy., 113

Yorkton, Saskatchewan, 30
Yellowhead Pass, 30

STATION INDEX

Canada

Alberta
Banff CPR, 13, 38, 40
Beiseker CNR and CPR, 3, 5
Berwyn ED&BCR (NAR) 76, 77
Bow Island CPR, 41, 42
Calgary CNR, 42-44
Calgary CPR, 3, 4, 7, 10, 16, 17, 42, 43, 97, 98
Claresholm CPR, 17
Codesa NAR, 6
Edmonton CNR, 3, 6, 19, 38, 39, 44, 80, 82, 102, 103
Edmonton CPR, 44
Edmonton NAR, 76, 105, 107
Edson CNR, 6, 65, 104
Faust NAR, 6
Galloway CNR, 61, 62
Gleichen CPR, 7, 8, 105
Hawkins GTPR, 6
High River CPR, 17
Innisfail C&ER (CPR) 26, 27
Innisfree CNR, 111
Irma GTPR, 6
Islay CNR, 104
Jarrow GTPR, 6
Jasper CNR, 80, 81
Kinsella GTPR, 6
Laggan (Lake Louise) CPR, 11, 13, 92
Lethbridge CPR, 26, 38
McLennan NAR, 76
Medicine Hat CPR, 2, 3, 7, 9, 38, 57, vi
Okotoks CPR, 87
Olds CPR, 10
Red Deer CPR, 38, 39, 57
Rycroft NAR, 76

St. Paul CNR, 61, 63
Smoky Lake CNR, 61, 62
South Edmonton (Strathcona) CPR, 26, 38
Stettler CNR, 58, 59
Three Hills GTPR, 70
Vegreville CNR, 6, 87, 89
Vermilion CNR, 58, 59
Wainwright GTPR, 65, 66
Waskatenau CNR, 87

British Columbia
Abbotsford BCER, 74
Agassiz CPR, 22, 23
Armstrong S&OR (CPR), 26, 27
Chilliwack CNR, 61, 62, 64
Clinton PGER (BCR) 76, 77
Cloverdale BCER, 74
Cranbrook CPR, 97
Dawson Creek PGER (BCR) 96
Elko CPR, 28
Enderby S&OR (CPR) 26
Fernie CPR, 28
Field CPR, 97, 98
Fort St. John PGER (BCR) 96
Glacier CPR, 12, 13
Great Central E&NR, 71
Hastings CPR, 17, 112
Hope CNR, 61
Houston CNR, 104
Huntingdon BCER, 74
Kamloops CNR, 84, 85
Kelowna CNR, 84
Langley BCER, 74
Maple Grove BCER, 74
Moberly CPR, 25
Nanaimo E&NR, 71, 72
New Westminster BCER, 71, 73
New Westminster CPR, 19, 20, 21
North Vancouver PGER (BCR) 105, 106

Parksville E&NR, 71, 72
Penticton CPR, 19, 94, 95
Port Alberni E&NR, 71
Port Moody CPR, 13, 112
Prairie BCER, 74
Prince Rupert GTPR, 31, 65
Revelstoke CPR, 84
Shalalth PGER, 96
Sicamous CPR, 19, 20
Smithers GTPR, 65
Vancouver BCER, 73, 74
Vancouver CNR, 50-52, 76, 84
Vancouver CPR, 3, 17, 18, 46-48
Vancouver GNR-NPR, 46
Vernon CPR, 6, 26, 38, 41, 57
Victoria E&NR, 71
West Summerland CPR, 84, 85

Manitoba
Brandon CNR, 6, 34-37, 84, 110
Brandon CPR, 13, 36, 37
Churchill CNR, 87, 99, 100
Dauphin CNR, 30, 38, 53
Gladstone CNR, 30
Laurier CNR, 53
Morden CPR, 22, 25
Neepawa CNR, 58
Pas CNR, 86, 87
Portage la Prairie CNR, 45
Portage la Prairie CPR, 14
Rivers GTPR, 65
St. Boniface CNR, 56, 57
St. Boniface CPR, 7, 10
St. Boniface GWWDR, 86, 87
Virden CNR, 22
Virden CPR, 22, 24
Winnipeg CNR Union, 3, 30, 34-36, 44, 65
Winnipeg CPR, 10, 11, 32-34
Winnipeg NPR, 14, 15

New Brunswick
McAdam Junction CPR, 112

Ontario
Claremont CPR, 7
Ernestown GTR, 67
Fort Frances CNR, 56, 57
Galt CPR, 112
Hamilton TH&BR, 96
Kenora CPR, 57, 112
Midland CNR, 104
Ottawa CPR, 112
Ottawa Union, 19
Pendleton CPR, 97
Port Arthur CNR, 38
Reditt GTPR, 65
Sioux Lookout GTPR, 65

Quebec
Montreal CNR, 99
Montreal CPR, 19, 112

Saskatchewan
Avonhurst GTPR, 70
Battleford CNR, 61
Biggar GTPR, 65
Borden CNR, 99
Coleville GTPR, 69, 109
Denholm CNR, 88, 90, 100

Estevan CNR, 61
Gilroy GTPR, 70
Hanley QALL&SR, 68
Kamsack CNR, 4
Lloydminster CPR, 85, 87
Melville GTPR, 65, 66, 84
Moose Jaw CPR, 3, 5, 18, 19, 78-80
Neilburg CPR, 88, 91
Nokomis GTPR, 68
Prince Albert CNR, 99
Regina Union (CPR), 3, 16, 17, 44, 83, 84, 97
Regina GTPR, 44, 65
Saskatoon CNR, 3, 6, 38, 84, 99, 101, 110
Saskatoon CPR Union, 26, 30, 38, 57
Saskatoon GTPR, 44
Saskatoon QALL&SR, 26
Scott CNR, 88, 90, 99
Unity GTPR, 65, 67
Wakaw GTPR, 70
Weyburn CNR, 87
Wilkie CPR, 40, 42

Yukon
Whitehorse WP&YR, 75

England
London, Euston, 34

United States
Burlington, Iowa CB&QR, 97
Hoboken, N.J. DL&WR, 112
New York, N.Y. Grand Central Station, 34
St. Louis, Mo. Union Station, 14